£14

Testing Time
MCC in the West Indies 1974

Testing Time

MCC in the West Indies 1974

Christopher Martin-Jenkins

Macdonald · London

Made and printed in Great Britain by
Redwood Burn Limited
Trowbridge & Esher

To Judy — for learning to live with my passion for cricket — and to James who in time, perhaps, will inherit it.

Contents

List of illustrations ix
Author's acknowledgments x
Foreword by E. W. Swanton xi

1 Prelude 1
2 Rain and runs 15
3 Instant drama 27
4 The run-out that never was 45
5 Sabina Park: a batsman's haven 53
6 Cricketing Houdinis: the Barbados Test 76
7 The tide turns at Georgetown 95
8 The decider: the second Trinidad Test 116
9 Analysis of a daylight robbery 141

Statistical survey by Bill Frindall 151
The teams 153
The averages 154
The scores 158
A statistician's diary 172

List of illustrations

Between pages 34 and 35

The first Test at Port of Spain: Boycott loses his cap to a Boyce bouncer; the rival captains are castled — Denness by Julien, Kanhai by Pocock; Boyce and Greig (in his 'old' style) about to deliver beneath the watchful gaze of umpire Sang Hue; incidents from the controversial Greig/Kallicharran 'run-out that never was' (*reproduced by courtesy of ITN news*).

Between pages 66 and 67

Variations on the sweep: Kallicharran at Bridgetown, Sobers at Port of Spain (first Test). Dennis Amiss, England's hero at Sabina Park, pulls another four in his mammoth 262 not out. England defend: Bob Willis in the first Test, Underwood in the second. Frank Hayes hooks during the first Test.

Between pages 98 and 99

The third Test at Bridgetown: Jameson hooks his first ball from Anderson Roberts into and out of the hands of long-leg; Lawrence Rowe off-drives Willis for four during his record-breaking 302, and finally succumbs to a catch at mid-wicket off Greig; Denness and Greig in contrasting styles struggle against the West Indian seam bowlers; Old is bowled first ball in the second innings; Greig cover-drives during his century; Sobers and Kanhai dispose of Boycott in the second innings.

Between pages 130 and 131

A Trinidadian spectator salutes Kallicharran's century in the first Test. The crowd at Queen's Park Oval, Port of Spain, and a panoramic view of the ground itself (scene of the only two decisive results in the series); weekend cricket in Barbados; rain stops play in Bridgetown (*photographs by Patrick Eagar*).

Between pages 162 and 163

The fourth Test at Georgetown: Jack Birkenshaw bowls Kallicharran for six; the author in the commentary box at the Bourda Oval. The fifth Test at Port of Spain: Dennis Amiss square-cuts off the front foot; Tony Greig leaps across the wicket to catch Clive Lloyd off his own bowling; the end of perhaps the last Test innings by Gary Sobers.

Author's acknowledgments

I should like to record my grateful thanks to Jim Swanton, both for his generous Foreword and for his kindly guidance to me over several years; to Jon Henderson of Reuters for his help during the writing of this book; to my employers, the BBC, for giving me the opportunity to report a fascinating tour; to Bill Frindall, who compiled the statistical survey; and not least to the English and West Indian cricketers for producing so much that was worth talking and writing about.

My thanks are also due to the following people, firms or newspapers who have supplied illustrations: Patrick Eagar; Hubert ('Sir John') Alexander of the *Trinidad Express*; Don Periana of the *Guyana Evening Post*; Wilkie Alleyne Associates of Barbados; *The Jamaican Daily Gleaner*; Sam. A. Apeji; and ITN news.

Foreword

It is a privilege to be asked to roll the wicket before a young author takes his first innings. In this case it is also a special pleasure since Christopher Martin-Jenkins's first job on coming down from Cambridge was to act as Assistant Editor of *The Cricketer* under my direction. In several years of close association I came quickly to admire both his industry and his extremely conscientious involvement in his work: likewise his affection for and close understanding of the game, which had their origins in a sporting family and a successful career at Marlborough where he captained the Eleven and headed the averages. At Cambridge he won his Crusader and took part in trials, and is today a highly useful club cricketer who has played for Surrey 2nd XI and who knows what it is to see three figures under his number on the scoreboard.

These qualifications are worth underlining, for the skills and subtleties of cricket, the ebb and sway of a match, and the critical assessment of players are best conveyed, in whatever form, by men who write or talk from first-hand knowledge, and who have aspired to a reasonable level of performance. Unhappily this is an age of much over-emphatic, unduly-personal games-writing, sometimes ungenerous to the point of scurrility. In such cases one more than suspects, as a rule, that the vehemence is in inverse ratio to the writer's acquaintance with the subject.

This cannot have been an easy book to write in several respects. Successful tour books need to be done quickly, for the interest, however keen it may be at the time, is largely ephemeral, and I know only too well what an effort of will is needed at the end of a hard and emotional Test day to sit down and commit the picture to paper while it is still fresh.

Again, it is more agreeable both to tell and to read a story of success, and here the author had all too little to enthuse over, apart from the exploits of Tony Greig and Dennis Amiss – until in the highly-charged, absorbing final Test Michael Denness's team succeeded in pulling their chestnuts out of the fire. I am reminded how at Melbourne twenty-three years ago F.R. Brown's MCC side at long last broke the sequence of Australian wins, and so gave me the title for my first tour book, *Elusive Victory*. That belated success in the fifth and final Test probably 'made' my book, for the publishers and myself. By the same token I'm sure this one will profit greatly from the recent happenings at Port of Spain.

To return to my opening simile, Mr Martin-Jenkins in these pages seems to me (from what I have seen of the book in typescript) to have played an auspicious opening innings. His strokes flow pleasantly off the middle of the bat. His method is sound and gives confidence. He is safe but never sticky. His judgment is good, too. Unlike England's open-ing batsmen he doesn't run anyone out – certainly not Denness, by the way, who seems to have suffered much harsh criticism. Happily this book will stand as a fair record when the journalism is forgotten.

Not least the author gives a refreshing personal sketch of the places and the people and the players of the West Indies. Barbados having been for many years my second home I turned with particular interest to the relevant chapter. Of the youngsters he says that they 'soon learn how to hit the ball, partly from instinct, partly from aping the famous players, whom they talk about as if they are members of the family': and of their elders, 'When they grow too old to play they watch the game and talk about it. Like anyone or anything held in great affection, cricket excites them, indulges them, intrigues them, irritates them, makes them laugh, and sometimes even makes them cry.' How well this depicts the nature of the sporting Bajan of all ages, who as a lover of cricket is second to none.

The BBC's recently-appointed cricket correspondent, I expect, has many tours ahead of him. I only hope therefore that this book is the first of a series under his name.

E. W. Swanton
Sandwich, April 1974

1
Prelude

The evening sun is bright, without a trace of the menacing rainclouds which have hovered fitfully over Port of Spain for days. Away in the northern hills which rise up behind the Queen's Park Oval, a few fleecy puffs play their shadows across the slopes. And out in the middle cricketers who have engaged in conflict for more than two months have arrived at the climax. The tension throughout this final day has been great, and now for the players, the watching crowd and the thousands listening throughout the Caribbean and far away across the Atlantic, it has become a test of nerves. West Indies, with their last pair together, need 27 runs to win both the match and the series. Lance Gibbs is facing, a man who has always jealously guarded his right to bat number eleven in the order, and who has rarely been threatened with the removal of that right. It seems inconceivable that England should not win the match now. Yet the ninth-wicket pair have just added 31 runs; Keith Boyce, a dangerous batsman capable of anything, is still at the crease; and the game has changed direction so often that one last sting in the tail would surprise no one. Geoff Arnold has the new ball in his hands. He has only one wicket to his credit in the entire series. A few loose balls now and he and his captain would be mercilessly chastised. He starts his long, straight, strong run-up, perspiration glinting on his forehead. Gibbs, sinewy, grey-haired and composed, stands ready. Arnold bowls, Gibbs swings blindly. The leg-stump is uprooted and, as if an Englishman, cartwheels in symbolic delight. Against the odds, against perhaps the

1

laws of natural justice, England have won the match and squared the series. The great escapers have brought off their *coup de grâce*.

The MCC tour of the West Indies in the early months of 1974 was seen, even before it began, as a yardstick by which the whole state of English cricket might be judged. Yet by the end of the tour it was curiously difficult to make any definitive judgment at all. After many disappointments, the honours of the series had been officially shared by means of a dramatic English victory in the final Test. But one left the West Indies blinking with amazement that a team blessed with relatively moderate talents should have overcome another which included several cricketers of genius. The simple reason was that in cricket, as in life, character and determination will go a long way towards making up for a lack of natural ability. But the story of the tour is not just the story of one remarkable victory. To put the whole tour in context one must look back first to the West Indian successes in England and the doubts they created about the general health of English cricket.

The game in England at the end of 1973 presented a curious paradox: on the one hand cricket was enjoying a boom in terms both of monetary profit and nationwide interest; on the other hand the England Test side had suffered at Lord's at the end of August a humiliating defeat – by an innings and 226 runs, the heaviest home defeat in their history.

It was even more curious, but certainly true, that the apparent decline in the standard of the national team was, in part at least, directly attributable to the rising fortunes of the seventeen professional County Clubs. A decade before, these clubs had been struggling in various degrees to make ends meet, and for some the terrible spectre of bankruptcy had loomed seriously; as recently as the winter of 1971 Surrey, one of the oldest and most illustrious of the County Clubs, had circulated their members with a desperate plea for immediate cash. The consequence of a slow response, they said, would be the fold-up of the club.

Yet by the end of 1972 Surrey, in common with all but two of the seventeen counties, was announcing a handsome profit. (The possibility of some 90% of the professional clubs announcing an annual profit is just one of the features of contemporary cricket which the football administrators view with envious longing.) In both the last two years the Test and County Cricket Board was able to make massive handouts to its affiliated clubs – in 1972 to the tune of £600,000; in 1973 almost as much.

In part the profit was a result of sponsorship by firms like John Player, Benson and Hedges, the Prudential Insurance Company and of course Gillette, whose relatively minute investment in cricket represents almost certainly the most triumphantly successful of all sporting sponsorships – successful both from the viewpoint of the sponsors, who have had enormous publicity and prestige from the Gillette Cup, and from *cricket's* viewpoint too, for it was the Gillette which in 1963 began the spate of one-day cricket competitions and brought back money, spectators and glamour to an ailing game.

But sponsorship and exciting, quick-result matches are only one side of the coin. The Test Match remains the biggest attraction and the noblest form of cricket. And one very good reason for the mammoth profit in 1972 and 1973 was the huge success of the home Test series against Australia, New Zealand and West Indies. England managed to retain the Ashes in the first of these series by the narrowest margin but it was men like Dennis Lillee, Bob Massie, Keith Stackpole and the Chappell brothers – all Australians – who performed most of the deeds which lived in the memory once the dust had settled. Again, from the 1973 season one remembered mainly the noble batting of Bevan Congdon, of Clive Lloyd, Gary Sobers, Alvin Kallicharran and Bernard Julien – and the bowling of Keith Boyce, Lance Gibbs and Vanburn Holder.

The cricket played by these men proved a tremendous attraction. The Ashes series alone was watched by over 417,000 spectators, and the estimated TV and radio audience aggregated well over 60 million. In addition, a staggering fifteen and a half million telephone calls in 1972 and nearly eighteen million in 1973 were received by the Post Office from eager followers in search of the latest score.

Every boom has its side-effects and this one was no exception. England's heavy defeats at the hands of the talented West Indians started the Jeremiahs wailing in their thousands. One-day cricket and the large numbers of overseas Test stars who filled the county teams were seen as the main reasons for the apparent decline in the national side. Bill-posters were once again taking on a martial appearance: 'England Surrender', 'Disaster Strikes', 'Illy's Army Routed' and the like. Elderly colonels were shooting themselves again. They even had a bomb scare at Lord's. English cricket was being written off once more, as it had been time and again since the performances of the national team had assumed an importance beyond the realms of mere sport.

England's decline in 1973 had perhaps been exaggerated. They still possessed some of the best seam bowlers in the world and in Alan Knott and Bob Taylor two of the most talented wicket-keepers anywhere. But over both the batting and the spin bowling hung heavy black question-marks. Under the brand new captaincy of a Scotsman, Mike Denness, could the English team restore morale by holding its own in the Caribbean? It was an intriguing question.

We know now that by dint of some remarkable

4

recoveries Denness's team did, in the end, precisely hold its own. Despite some shocking batting collapses and much vain toil by a disappointing set of bowlers, the steel and character traditionally displayed by English cricket teams abroad enabled the side to save two matches which seemed hopelessly lost, and then to win the last and most important game. Yet, as will be seen, only two players could truly feel proud of what they had contributed to an enigmatic tour.

The team selected in September (it can be found in full at the end of the book) had one or two surprising selections and notable omissions. The young Derbyshire swing bowler Mike Hendrick was preferred to John Snow of Sussex, who had taken a record 27 wickets on the 1968 MCC tour of the West Indies, whilst the Warwickshire opening batsman John Jameson was preferred to one or two more experienced Test cricketers, notably John Edrich, Colin Cowdrey and Brian Luckhurst. But, as usual, most of the discussion about the team (before, during and after the tour) concerned the choice of captain.

Denness had been made captain of England at the end of the 1973 season amidst the sort of controversy which invariably affects that appointment – one which excites as much public discussion as the leader of a political party or the choice of England's football team manager. In one sense Denness's elevation was no surprise, for he had been vice-captain to Tony Lewis in the East the winter before, where, like Lewis, he had done an excellent job. Lewis, officially next in line to the succession once Ray Illingworth was pronounced unfit to rule, was not a serious candidate now because persistent injury had allowed him very little cricket after one unhappy Test Match against New Zealand early in the summer.

In another sense the choice of Denness was illogical. He had begun the 1973 season with a burst of handsome scoring which made him a certain selection in the minds of everyone but the selectors. Then, on the morning of the Test Trial at Hove, he withdrew from the match because of a minor back-strain. Four days later, he made a hundred for Kent. People said that Denness was not selected because this century proved to the selectors that there had been nothing wrong with him — ignorant comment indeed, because the First Test team had in fact been chosen on the Friday of the Hove match, before Denness had even put his pads on. Perhaps there was just a thought, nonetheless, that he had not wanted to risk marring his chances by having an unsuccessful trial. In the event, Graham Roope rose to the occasion with a colourful century and Frank Hayes chose this important match to show his immense potential. Between them, these two were to keep Denness out of the England side all summer long. Even in the hour of greatest need, when England had to produce a win at Lord's to save their faces and the rubber, Illingworth and the other selectors persevered with another Kent player, Brian Luckhurst.

When Luckhurst and, more important, Illingworth failed, Denness suddenly became a prime candidate again, though it is worth remembering that he was by no means the only one. Some wanted Lewis, despite his lack of fitness and of practice. Others wanted a completely new broom, someone with the old dash of amateur adventure in his blood — Mike Brearley of Middlesex perhaps, or Richard Gilliatt of the new County Champions Hampshire. In the opposing camp to this 'University' school of thought were those who believed that if Illingworth had lost his magic, no one could replace him more suitably than Brian Close. An ironic choice indeed he would have been! For Close had lost the England captaincy in far more controversial circumstances before the last West Indies tour of 1968.

But the great majority of cricket followers in England still believed that Ray Illingworth was the best man for the job. This friendly, open character would not have let anyone down as a diplomat – a consideration which cannot be overlooked when the captain of a touring side is being chosen. What mattered therefore was whether Illingworth could truly be considered on merit as an all-rounder and, equally important, whether he had lost his touch as a captain. He was probably a better bowler now, in his 41st year, than he had been when rudely exposed on the unhelpful pitches of the Caribbean in 1959. Certainly, he was a better batsman too. It is true that there were beginning to be doubts about his ability to produce the goods in a crisis as he had so often done with such coolness and resource while he had been captain. (He was one of the comparatively few examples of a cricketer apparently inspired by the responsibilities of captaincy to improve his own performances, rather than allowing himself to be adversely affected by all its cares and problems.) But it was the issue of his captaincy alone that was most crucial. My own view is that Ray Illingworth was shell-shocked. How else could a man of his vast cricket experience lay the blame for defeat by an innings and 226 runs at the door of the pitch? It was a pitch of uneven bounce, he said. Perhaps so, but the West Indies had made 652 for 8 declared on it, and a few days later the same strip of tired white turf produced plenty of runs in the Gillette Cup Final. The unavoidable fact was that Ray Illingworth and his team had been soundly thrashed by a side more talented in batting, bowling and fielding. For this, the ageing General of 'Dad's Army' had to carry full responsibility. The Illingworth era was over and the selectors turned to Denness.

Mike Denness was not an unreasonable choice for the task which lay ahead. At the age of 32 he had been given less Test Match experience than he might have had a right to expect in a lean period for English batting. For this solid citizen, born and educated in Scotland, had always looked a good player, with a full range of attractive strokes. In the Orient under Tony Lewis he had played with great consistency without producing the really big innings that a complete Test batsman should. But he had one great advantage on his side: he was used to success. Unlucky he may have been to be left out of England's team all summer, but it was a positive asset that he should thus have avoided the mauling, physical and psychological, which his colleagues suffered. He came freshly to the job in hand, head high after a season of continued and continuous success at the helm for Kent, who had won two of the four County competitions.

The Kent side under Denness always appeared a formidable all-round team, never more impressive than when in the field, every man prepared to throw at the stumps whenever the slightest chance of a run-out occurred, and most of the team capable of taking the most outrageous catches. Certainly much of Kent's spirit and success was due to Colin Cowdrey and to the manager Leslie Ames, but after taking over from Cowdrey in 1972 Denness had built successfully on the firm foundations. He deserved his big chance.

Once the selectors had decided to dispense with Illingworth, his successor – whoever was chosen – was bound to be something of a gamble. Brian Close would have been one in a diplomatic sense, for in times of trouble or tribulation his past could always have been held against him. But as captain of Derrick Robins's team which, with two coloured players, made a successful tour of South Africa at the end of 1973, he showed what might have been. This literally battle-scarred veteran, who had played for England as a gauche but brilliant 18-year-old and whose career thereafter had risen and fallen like the graph of a patient with malaria, led an assorted team with shrewdness, determination and considerable success on the field and with tact and typical firmness off it.

But Close, always a colourful and, in his noblest moments, a great cricketer, had proved his point too late. In any case, the selectors had every right to ask what logic there would have been in dispensing with one veteran — Illingworth — only to replace him with another — Close. It would have been quite as big a gamble in the other direction to have chosen Brearley or Gilliat. Either would probably have done a good job (and either could yet be asked to do it in future) but neither had achieved enough in the tough school of County cricket to merit a Test place. A man has to be a truly outstanding leader, especially in modern cricket, if he is to overcome the disadvantage of not being worth his place on playing merit alone.

So, as the Tories turned to Sir Alec Douglas-Home after Harold Macmillan's abdication, England's ever-cautious selectors chose the 'safe' candidate, Mike Denness, to succeed the weary Ray Illingworth. Part of the fascination of the MCC tour lay in the way that this slickly dressed, quiet-spoken man, whose education at Ayr Academy had coincided with that of two Scottish Internationals from other sports — Ian Ure and Ian McLauchlan — faced his responsibilities and solved his problems. At the time, he was something of an anonymous figure, known to those who report the game as one of the less approachable of the County captains — if only because, every inch a canny Scot, he had an agent who tended to ask money for verbal gems which others might have dropped more freely!

Nor had it endeared him to the bulk of the scoop-conscious Press when someone — not Denness himself — had leaked the news of his appointment to one or two privileged men of the media. Such things mean little to the average newspaper reader but in Fleet Street they can sometimes mean professional life or death. Elaborating a little on this important issue, one feels that there is still room for improvement in the area of communicating certain cricket matters to the media, excellently though the authorities at Lord's have striven to improve their image. Cricketers, by and large, are not fools. They are not so naive as to be unaware of the difference between straight cricket talk and the passing on of information likely to be inflammatory. It is precisely the suppression of information which sometimes leads to mischievous cricket stories appearing in the Press. If the facts are made clear quickly and openly, dangerous speculation or damaging comment can be avoided.

Cricket authorities in England are still inclined to suffer from reaction to the traumatic South African hullaballoo of 1968–70, which is perhaps only natural. I can, however, see no harm in having rather less restrictive contracts for cricketers in future, provided players clearly appreciate that they may talk only about cricketing matters in the strictly technical sense, leaving controversial issues to the Captain or the Manager. There is enormous goodwill in the game of cricket, but unfortunately not always complete trust. Secrecy breeds suspicion and often malicious gossip. (Perhaps, though, this theory goes against the grain of Fleet Street, which, after all, is the home of gossip! Perhaps, too, part of the charm of reporting cricket lies in the cloak-and-dagger atmosphere which occasionally prevails; the appointment of the England captain being a perennial case in point.)

One further aspect of the England/West Indies series of 1973 must be recalled before the narrative of the extraordinary tour which followed can be fully understood. The three-match series was outstanding chiefly because of the general magnificence of the West Indian cricket at the Oval and at Lord's. In the first Test the West Indies won a resounding victory which made the long lean period that had gone before all the more remarkable. The shrewd, determined captaincy of Kanhai, the return of the great Sobers, and the growing maturity of Boyce, Julien and Kallicharran all had a part to play in the joyous win at the Oval and the even greater triumph at Lord's. But both these matches and, to a greater extent, the dull draw at Edgbaston which divided them, were spoiled by some unpleasant moments on and off the field.

Hitherto cricket crowd problems had been largely confined to other countries. But at the Oval England sensed a whiff of smoke which could well have turned into fire in certain circumstances. Ever-mindful of economics, the Surrey Club had ordered far too few policemen to be assured of complete control over a large crowd, should it have become unruly. In the event the worst that happened was a number of disorderly but generally good-humoured invasions of the field. The weather was dry and the pitch did not suffer much, though it might easily have done. The most seriously injured party was probably Frank Hayes, who, having completed an auspicious hundred in his first Test Match, was copiously kissed in the middle of the pitch before thousands of spectators by an exuberant, bearded West Indian.

In the joy of victory such excesses of enthusiasm were forgiven easily enough, and even if one suspected at the time a slight undertone of racial feeling beneath the jubilation of some of the celebrating supporters, and a certain affinity with the aggressive instincts so often displayed by football 'fans', the atmosphere was still overwhelmingly good-natured.

The irony of the Edgbaston Test which followed was that, while the crowds were excellently behaved and impeccably controlled – not an errant foot disturbed the carefully protected turf – the players themselves let the game down. Somehow it was an ill-starred Test Match from the outset. Rohan Kanhai has denied that he was playing for a draw from the moment the coin was tossed, and I am sure he would have tried to win the match if he could have done so without risk of losing it. The fact is, though, that after West Indies had won the toss on a good wicket, Roy Fredericks scored a century of such pain-staking caution that a draw was always the most likely result. The dullness of much of the West Indian cricket and the dilatory, confused, lack-lustre English batting on the third day (which had begun with England in a strong position) was nothing new in Test cricket, indeed deserved only to be forgotten. What could not be forgotten so easily was the unpleasant little storm in a teacup which came to be known as the 'Fagg Affair'.

The trouble began with the unfortunate Geoff Boycott as a central figure. Despite his earnest and well-meaning efforts to brighten his public image, this great batsman has seemed to carry controversy around with him like a shadow almost from the start of his career. Often the fault has not been his own and in this particular case he was almost certainly blameless.

The catalyst of the affair was the West Indian reaction to Umpire Arthur Fagg's decision to give Boycott not out following a loud appeal for a catch behind the wicket. I saw what happened clearly from the pavilion end where Boycott was batting and my most vivid impression was of Keith Boyce, the bowler, delivering his appeal, vehemently enough, but not until *after* he had heard the appeal from the fielders behind the wicket. The difference was a mere split-second, but it was enough to suggest that Boyce had not immediately believed that he had got England's key batsman caught behind. In the light of this, Fagg's decision of 'not out' was wholly understandable. There are times in cricket when decisions like this can seem obviously 'out' from one end, apparently 'not out' from the other. For what it is worth, the television commentator Jim Laker, thanks to the marvellous but also mischievous modern invention, the Video playback, had a privileged opportunity to see the incident in question over and over again, and believed in the end that Fagg had been right.

Whether he was right or not, of course, was not in any case the primary issue. The decision was made, and every cricketer is brought up to believe that the umpire's decision is final. Unfortunately Rohan Kanhai, succumbing to the intense pressures of his job rather than remembering his responsibilities, protested ostentatiously before the eyes not only of the live crowd but of all the TV viewers.

Apparently this initial reaction was not the end of the matter and further complaints were made to the umpire by the fielding side in the final session of play. The result was that when Fagg was questioned by pressmen as he prepared to leave the ground that evening, he let forth his own protest. His was not a personal attack on Kanhai but a general condemnation of gamesmanship in the modern game and of course it made headlines — headlines which grew bolder when Fagg, upset by the storm to which his own words had contributed, threatened to leave the match.

In the event Alan Oakman, the Warwickshire coach and a sometime first-class umpire, stood in his stead for one over on the third morning. A West Indian statement of faith in Fagg's umpiring had persuaded him to return, but no apology was made. An apology should have been made. By over-reacting as they did both Kanhai and Fagg had allowed pride to get the better of humility.

It was an unfortunate start to what turned out to be the grimmest day's Test cricket of the summer, in which the over-rate fell to thirteen an hour before lunch when England could score only 40 runs, and it illustrated clearly how high emotions can rise in Test cricket. It also served as a salutary reminder, in the light of previous troubles during Test Matches in the West Indies, of how incidents on the field can spread to the crowd and become magnified out of all proportion. A storm in a teacup it may have been. But one felt at the time that had it happened six months later it *might* have turned into a Caribbean hurricane. Perhaps it was a blessing in disguise that the trouble should have happened in the relatively apathetic atmosphere of Edgbaston rather than in the midst of the passionately committed spectators of the West Indies, because the MCC tour which followed was the first since the war to pass without a serious crowd incident, and the traditional West Indian enthusiasm never once got out of hand or turned to unpleasantness.

There was one more unsavoury incident to come in the 1973 Tests, though it was to be quickly forgotten in the post-mortems: hardly surprisingly, since the West Indian cricket was so brilliant and the English cricket so demoralised that there were more important things to discuss. All the same, the buffeting which Geoff Boycott received after his twilight dismissal on the Saturday of the Lord's Test — the day of the notorious, abortive bomb scare when the ground was laboriously evacuated during the afternoon — will never be forgotten by Boycott himself. He was surrounded and physically bustled by mocking spectators, when all he wanted to do was to return to the sanctuary of the pavilion as quickly as possible. Bomb scares and batsmen assaulted: it was all very out of tune with cricket's image as a game of peace and dignity!

2
Rain and Runs

There are many things to be said in favour of short cricket tours. Despite the advent of jet-air travel, which has cut down the length of tours considerably compared with the leisurely ocean-going days of old, the modern Anglo-Australian visits (for instance) are still too long. A certain staleness is bound to affect players who are continually on the go for five months, especially when, in the case of the English professional, there is only the briefest respite between the rigours of summer and the pressures of a winter cricket tour.

England's disastrous performances at the end of 1973 had been partially attributable to the accumulative effects of too much cricket. Tony Greig, to give the most prominent example, had become a pale, emaciated warrior following nineteen successive Test Matches without a break. His keen spirit was still telling his body to go through the motions, but it was a spirit with its competitive edge blunted, and a body which was just too tired to carry out its orders to maximum efficiency. Yet when Greig left London with his fifteen colleagues on a mild, grey January afternoon, he was in every way a fitter man. Sun-tanned from a holiday in South Africa (as also were Geoff Boycott and Bob Willis, who had both been coaching in the isolated Republic) Greig had added well over a stone to his weight.

Mike Denness had said on his appointment that what his side most needed was a good rest. This they had got, and the batteries were now fully re-charged. The irony was that, with five Test Matches to be fitted into three months, only three weeks were available for practice and acclimatisation before the first Test at Port of Spain — and, of all things in the sunny Caribbean, it rained.

In the nature of things, any short cricket tour is more susceptible to disruption by bad weather than a long one is, but the West Indies in January *ought* to be sunny. When only two-and-a-half hours' play was possible in the first three-day match against the Windward Islands, the likes of Frank Hayes must have felt like saying: 'Come back Manchester, all is forgiven' — especially as he personally found time to make a duck during that brief period of play.

In fact, there is a greater risk of rain in the banana island of St Lucia than in most West Indian islands at this time of year, but the irony was all the sharper for the fact that the MCC seemed to have brought their rainclouds with them. Whilst they were staring gloomily at grey skies, itching for match practice like dogs for their dinner, the big West Indian names in other parts of the Caribbean were flexing their muscles in the sun. While MCC struggled to 124 for 5 between the showers, Lawrence Rowe was making 204 in a Jamaican total of 483 against Guyana in the Shell Shield and Guyana were replying with 478, of which Alvin Kallicharran contributed 197 and Clive Lloyd 134. Meanwhile, in Bridgetown, Keith Boyce was adding bowling figures of 5 for 56 to a breezy innings of 60, and, to add insult to injury, a certain Vanburn Holder, who usually goes in at number ten for his adopted county, Worcestershire, was making 122 for Barbados against Trinidad.

But while these old faithfuls were playing their way into form, the West Indian selectors — Clyde Walcott, J.K.Holt and Joe Solomon — decided to use the President's XI match (the equivalent game to the one between the MCC and the touring side in England towards the end of May) to blood some young talent. The combination of a young, scratch side, the benign quality of the Kensington Oval wicket and the arrival of some fine weather (at last) allowed the MCC to wipe out the memory of six fruitless days in St Lucia and to produce a most encouraging performance.

The only pluses to come out of the St Lucian trip had been Dennis Amiss's fine century in the one-day match against the Combined Leeward-Windward Islands (which MCC lost by five runs) and the brisk 39 scored by John Jameson in what there was of the second match. But in Barbados Geoff Boycott made 261 not out, Amiss another century, Fletcher an attractive 70 and, in the second innings, Jameson, opening the batting, made 87 at a rate of better than a run a minute. Best of all, MCC, after declaring at 511 for 4 — the very size of the total did much for their morale — all but won the game. They bowled the President's XI out cheaply in the first innings, with Geoff Arnold, who had incidentally taken a wicket with the very first ball of the tour in Castries, collecting five wickets for 44. Then after being frustrated, rather ominously, by two young left-handers, Baichan from Guyana and Chang from Jamaica, they suddenly broke through again in the second innings with Bob Willis taking four wickets in the innings and Chris Old three. Only a stubborn last-wicket partnership between Baichan, who carried his bat heroically for 139, and Anderson Roberts, the promising young fast bowler now on the Hampshire staff, saved the day for the President's XI.

Looking at the scorecard after the event, it is hard to recall that Boycott's 261 not out (which topped his previous highest score by a single run) was seen in some quarters as something other than a triumph. Certainly it was a magnificent portrayal of his near-flawless technique, his insatiable appetite for runs and his admirable dedication and concentration. But, as I have said before, Boycott and controversy frequently go hand in hand. No one criticised the first stage of his innings, when on the opening day of the match he made 135 not out out of 283 for 2. It had not been Boycott at his dominating best, but the important thing was that a major score was on the board against the name of England's major batsman in a major match.

The case against the second stage of his innings, in which he all but doubled his score with no great acceleration, was put best by E. W. Swanton, who wrote in the *Daily Telegraph*:

'Starting the day at 284 for 2, MCC were already assured of as many runs as they wanted. It was a matter of who was going to get the chance of making them . . .

'One wondered how some of Boycott's distinguished predecessors would have reacted to this situation of a side with scarcely any match practice behind them and only one match to come before the first Test . . . . Cricketers have got out without fuss or ostentation for the sake of their friends and the side since time began. Boycott, however, is a law to himself . . . .'

Which of course is just the point. Boycott is an independent man, a proud professional employed to make runs, with no intention of ever sacrificing his wicket in any cause unless he is forced to. In this case he was under orders from his captain to go on as long as he wished, which was, of course, for ever. No doubt, viewed from certain angles, this was a selfish effort. But the psychological importance of the innings was incalculable. Here was Boycott, the nearest thing to Bradman since Bradman, rapping out a warning to the whole Caribbean that he had arrived and was ready to conquer. And here were the MCC announcing with a clarion call that they were nobody's pushovers.

When you arrive in the Caribbean from a cold English January, the first breath of air is like that from a hot oven.

The cool of the air-conditioned aircraft is replaced by a warm breeze and if, like any good, sober Englishman, you arrive clad in suit and tie, the clammy feel of the palms of your hands soon tells you that you are overdressed.

Trinidad, where the MCC journeyed next, is one of the wealthier Caribbean islands, with natural resources which include that most precious of modern commodities, oil. Port of Spain, where the team stayed, and which is the home of the beautiful and impressive Queen's Park Oval, is a stately old colonial town, with wide streets, spacious shuttered houses under red corrugated iron roofs, elegant palms and spreading, majestic Saman trees. Life here moves at a slow and dignified pace, the dining-room service in the old Victorian hotel where the players stayed being no exception. Some members of the party who expected 'beautiful hotels, white sandy beaches lined with palms, and calypso bands' were disillusioned, no doubt misled by the glossy travel brochures. One player even expected to find the lush turf of England reproduced in the harsher outfields of the West Indies. In general, however, the MCC cricketers found Trinidad friendly, if cautious. The people did not turn up in their thousands for the island's four-day game, preferring to spare their dollars and to listen on their transistors to the progress of the match while preparing for the excitement and big-match atmosphere of the forth-coming Test.

But for the cricket connoisseur there was plenty of interest in the game which preceded the Test. Denness won an important toss; MCC packed their side with practice-hungry batsmen; Arnold, Willis and Pocock were rested, the unfortunate Taylor was left out again, and Knott, who had much to do to justify his preferential treatment, was chosen as wicket-keeper once more to give him batting practice. Poor man, he got a good one from Julien in his first over and made nought in the first innings followed by a diffident 11 in the second. But poor Taylor too. Here he was, still without a game after four matches. His only match practice had been in the benefit games for Kanhai and Gibbs, and in these he had kept wicket as impeccably as ever, as well as making 68. At Trinidad, where the pitch demanded spin bowling and a wicket-keeper outstanding up at the stumps, there was a good case for giving Taylor his chance. But it never seemed to be seriously considered.

The first day showed again how swiftly fortunes can change in cricket. The match had begun with John Jameson very much the favourite to bat at number three in the first Test Match, and there was already talk too that Geoff Boycott should drop down the order and come in instead at number four. Tony Greig expressed this view shortly before the first Test. 'I think he should have gone in four against Lillee and Massie in 1972. There's such a danger that if your leading batsman gets out early, everyone gets into a panic and thinks the bowling is impossible. Before you know where you are you've got another collapse on your hands.'

Greig's feeling was that if another opening pair could weather the early storm, the rest of the batting would be that much more confident and Boycott would have been free to come in with the pressure off and the awful feeling dispelled that he had to succeed if the whole side was not to fail.

It was certainly an interesting theory but, assuming that it was not to be tested this early in the tour, Amiss and Boycott were still the established opening pair, and other batting places had to be found for Denness and Fletcher, which left Hayes and Jameson to fight for the final batting place. Jameson began the Trinidad match a clear favourite, having added a rapid 87 to his auspicious opening knock of 39 and being just the man, it seemed, to take the attack to the opposition. But the adamantine surface at Bridgetown was one thing, the sandy-coloured Port of Spain pitch, with its clear tendency to favour the spinners, was quite another, and it was Hayes who recovered from his early low scores to play the best innings for MCC.

Denness had again won the toss, so his batsmen were assured of a good look at the much-discussed wicket, and this is precisely what Amiss and Boycott got as they meandered in ones and twos before a subdued crowd, scattered in colourful blobs beneath the handsome spreading Saman trees. Then Bernard Julien, fighting for his Test place, whipped a perfectly pitched inswinger through Boycott's tentative half-cock forward shot and, small though it was, the crowd erupted in noise as his middle stump sagged back like a drunken man. A spectator in a crimson shirt, all brown eyes and smiling teeth, ran out from the concrete stand by the commentary box, looked up and shouted at me: 'Englishman – what I tell you, man? Boycott a rabbit, a bloody *rabbit*!'

Jameson marched proudly in at number three, back like a guardsman's, pigeon chest puffed out, stroked his first ball for two, slashed the next for four and then holed out in the next over at cover. It was the Keith Stackpole approach, the Colin Milburn approach, but Jameson had come and gone like a sudden breeze on a sultry day, and one was left thinking: is this really how an England number three should play?

Hayes, in contrast, was discretion itself. Not cautious, note, but discreet. He moved his feet to the spinners, stroked the ball cleanly, watched it carefully, had plenty of time. While the others struggled, sometimes painfully, against Trinidad's talented young spinners, Jumadeen and Imtiaz Ali (left-arm orthodox and leg-spin respectively), Hayes stayed in control until beaten at last by Imtiaz. In the absence of Inshan, being kept in hand for the Test, Imtiaz was impressive, with a looping flight, sharp spin and lively bounce. Moreover he varied his attack constantly and Amiss, Hayes and Greig all fell to him. But Amiss, with innings of 34 and 86, continued his successful start to the tour, while Hayes added a cultured 88 to his first innings 47 to make absolutely sure of his Test place.

Greig had innings of 70 and 100 not out, his first successes of the tour, and it was he and Jack Birkenshaw who held the stage from the English viewpoint for much of the rest of the match. When the crowd saw Greig, this great fair-haired pole of a man, shape up to face his first ball with his peculiar early pick-up, they roared with laughter. 'His bat is too small,' they said, grinning to one another. It seemed that Greig would capture their imagination as he had the Indians' in the previous winter, but he blotted his copybook for the first time later on the second day when appealing with excessive vehemence against the Trinidad captain Deryck Murray. Murray had not scored at this stage of his innings and it had certainly looked one of those l.b.w.'s which can almost be given out from the boundary. But the umpire, Gosein, only gives l.b.w.'s against *any* batsman when he is entirely convinced that the man is out, and that is as it should be. Greig remembered his responsibilities in time but the incident rankled. Next day the *Trinidad Guardian* ran a screaming headline: 'GREIG LOSES POPULARITY AT OVAL', followed by the lead story which gave a clear warning to MCC in general and to Greig, whose South African connections he is never allowed to forget, in particular:

'Yesterday was the day when South-African born Tony Greig stood tall with two fine performances, but later lost most of his popularity when Umpire Ralph Gosein turned down his appeal for leg before against Deryck Murray, the Trinidad captain . . . . Greig's appeal and show of annoyance, supported by many of the MCC players, could well be the start of a psychological "war" against the West Indies umpires.'

Nonsense, perhaps. Exaggerated, certainly. But that is what happens on overseas cricket tours. Another account described how Greig stamped his foot when Murray was given not out. I saw the incident differently but he certainly lingered excessively with his arms in the air when it was quite apparent that his appeal had been turned down. It is all too easy to criticise players in the heat of the middle from the cool of the boundary, but as vice-captain and with his special background Greig had to be doubly careful not to offend. Murray, incidentally, tried to get his own back by using every possible means to deny Greig his century at the end of the game. (It was his own scrupulously patient innings of 148 which ensured that Trinidad would not lose the match.)

In other respects Greig had a mature appreciation of his job as vice-captain, believing that he must support his captain all the way, advise him when asked to do so but not seek to overstep his limits. He saw himself too as the means by which the captain might be made aware of any kind of discontent in the party. It was not difficult to imagine Greig himself captaining an England team in the future, but he was soon to jeopardize his chances of doing so in a much more serious incident, which will be dealt with fully in the next chapters.

Jack Birkenshaw was the other English player who captured the imagination of Trinidad. At the end of a day of mediocre batting in the match against the island, he came in, neat and dapper in his white floppy sun-hat, to play an easy, cultured innings at number nine. During its course he was struck on the fore-finger of his left hand and an X-ray at lunchtime on the second day revealed that a bone was cracked. It didn't stop Birkenshaw hitting five fours and one splendid six to finish with 53 not out. Then, with fingers strapped, he wheeled his way cheerfully through 39 overs of the Trinidad first innings, taking 3 for 82. The injury was unfortunate indeed, for he must have had a good chance of selection for the first Test. It was the Test with which everyone became concerned as the Trinidad match ran out of time and petered out into an aimless draw.

The two teams were announced, after much speculation, on the day before the Test. In the previous Caribbean season the West Indies had chosen three spin bowlers for both the Trinidad Tests against Australia. Inshan Ali and Gibbs had played in both with a different left-arm orthodox spinner to add variety – Elquemedo Willett in the Third Test, Raphick Jumadeen in the last. But after the successes of the West Indian faster bowlers in England it was always likely that even on the slowly paced Port of Spain pitch the West Indian selectors would choose a more balanced attack with at least two quick bowlers. With Rowe from Jamaica now fully fit again (before his double century in the Shell Shield he had injured a hip, and he had to pull out of the President's XI match against MCC at the last moment) there was little doubt that he would become Fredericks' opening partner in place of his island captain Maurice Foster. This left one very awkward choice: whom to leave out of the trio of Boyce, Holder and Julien. Holder and Boyce had played immense parts in beating England the year before with their hostile fast bowling. Julien was a young man of wonderful all-round talents, he would be playing on his home ground in Port of Spain and he had done his stock a lot of good by spreadeagling Boycott's stumps. Boycott had shown a weakness against left-arm over-the-wicket bowling in the past – most notably of course against Garfield Sobers himself. So Julien played and Vanburn Holder was the unlucky omission.

England had a similar choice to make between seam bowlers, though they raised a good many eyebrows by naming three fast bowlers in a squad of twelve. This seemed to open up the possibility of their playing at Port of Spain with four seam bowlers – Arnold, Willis, Old and Greig – and only one spinner – either Underwood or Pocock. It would have been sheer madness to have done this when all recent evidence suggested a slow wicket of low bounce and a definite tendency to help the spinners. Sanity prevailed and it was Arnold of the three fast men who was left out. The news that England's leading opening bowler of the past few seasons had been dropped did not emerge until the morning of the match, though he had been quietly told the night before. For 'Oss' there was considerable consolation in knowing that he was virtually certain of selection for the later Test Matches.

On paper there was never any doubting the superior strength of the West Indian XI. Their batting line-up alone was truly formidable, with the experience of men like Kanhai, Sobers and Lloyd carefully blended with the youthful genius of Rowe, Kallicharran and Julien, and, dotted about the order here and there, players like Murray or Fredericks who would shine in many Test sides but who in this one were nothing special. Seven of the team had made Test hundreds; and Keith Boyce, with a reputation as a decimator of attacks, was to bat as low as number nine.

England's batting, on the other hand, was short of true class. On the previous Caribbean tour of 1968, Cowdrey, Graveney, Barrington, Edrich, D'Oliveira and Milburn had made up a batting combination to fear. I almost forgot to add Boycott, who marched like a royal conqueror through that tour but who had made strides sideways rather than forwards since, as the responsibility on his shoulders began to increase and take its toll. When Boycott failed nowadays, a state of collapse seemed to be endemic in the England camp, though as often as not in the Illingworth era the bowlers (sometimes in the guise of tail-end batsmen) baled their colleagues out. But now, with that galaxy of West Indian batsmen at the ready, the bowlers could not be expected to take the main burden again. To survive in this series, England *had* to make plenty of runs. Yet the start they were about to make at Port of Spain could hardly have been more disastrous.

3
Instant Drama

February 2nd, 1974. A day long awaited in Trinidad. Indeed throughout the Caribbean and by thousands of cricket-followers in England too. It dawns through a slate-grey sky and, waking up and looking at that sky, you feel you might indeed be in England. But out in the open air the temperature is very different, for the morning is stifling, uncomfortably humid.

Since break of day, Trinidad's multi-racial community seems to have been converging almost to a man on the Queen's Park Oval. Outside the ground, guarded by high walls topped with barbed wire and broken glass, mounted police are keeping sure control of an orderly, good-humoured, expectant crowd. Once inside, the din has to be heard to be believed, a cacophony of unbridled excitement, quite unlike the forced, regimented noise of English football supporters or a Welsh rugby crowd.

A high wire fence surrounds the playing area but it blots out not a decibel of sound or atmosphere. The crowds in the West Indies are a part of the game itself. They cannot and will not be cut off from it. It is a daunting audience to play before.

Ten o'clock. Half an hour to go before play begins, and still the sky hangs heavy overhead. A tremendous roar and a deep rumble of thousands of clapping hands as Kanhai, smart maroon blazer beneath iron grey hair, leads out a nervous-looking Denness to the middle to toss. The pitch is unbelievably flat, rolled and rolled by an eager team of some twenty bare-footed groundsmen to a state of concrete perfection. Is there moisture there, despite the

27

covers, after yesterday's heavy rain? Or will this clinging, burdensome atmosphere be in the minds of the captains as they toss? If England are to field, should Arnold have been in the side to exploit these conditions? But *will* England be in the field? Kanhai has won the toss and somehow the crowd seems to know instinctively at once, for another deep rumbling applause breaks out below the yells and screams, the bells and whistles. 'I'll let you know,' says Kanhai, and briskly he strides off again towards the pavilion, there to disappear for a quick discussion with Sobers and Gibbs.

Soon the fateful decision is made. Insertion. England are to be put to the test at once. Boyce, Julien and Sobers are to be given the new ball. In this atmosphere it will swing for sure. How will Boycott fare? Will he resist the temptation to hook before he is set? He must, for there will be bouncers. Inevitably there will be bouncers. And Amiss: how much does that wonderfully consistent start to his tour mean now? Now is when it really matters. Can he control the short, rising ball on the off stump? To the Englishman familiar with the dreadful uncertainty of English batting in recent seasons, these questions circle anxiously round the mind as the umpires, little Sang Hue, dapper and dignified in white hat, coat and shoes, and the Indian-looking Gosein, cool and detached despite his recent publicity, approach the middle.

Now Kanhai again, and at his shoulder, to a delighted roar of recognition, comes King Garfield, easing his way across the grass with that familiar loping, vulpine walk, a faded cream-yellow shirt open at the chest. Little pockets of applause break out as different parts of the crowd recognise their own particular favourites: Clive Lloyd, the 'great, gangling begoggled supercat'; little Alvin Kallicharran of the dancing feet; the new boy Lawrence Rowe, wearing his maroon cap like a jockey and looking like a photograph of the great George Headley; and the local favourites, Bernard Julien and Inshan Ali.

Finally, the batsmen. Dennis Amiss, squarely built with a rolling gait, England's royal blue cap pulled well over his eyes which are facing the ground as he walks. Will he be the bold, assertive batsman he can be? Or the diffident, prodding Amiss of old? And Boycott: no eyes down for him. His head is proudly up, taking in the dull light and the eager, baying crowd. Will he fail? He mustn't. In these waters of the Caribbean Nelson himself once sailed and sheltered his fleet. England expects . . . But it is Geoffrey Boycott of whom they expect most.

But Boycott did fail. England as a team failed lamentably. And the West Indies took up their triumphant march exactly where they had stopped at Lord's in September.

Ironically, though, that match had been won in Caribbean conditions of hot sun and a hard, fast wicket. But at Port of Spain on this first day of the new series, clouds were billowing angrily over the northern hills at the back of the ground and in the oppressive, clammy atmosphere the ball moved around as it does in a sea fret at Hove. They were difficult conditions in which to bat, and whereas on most pitches in a five-day Test Match the captain considers the possibility of the pitch breaking up towards the end of the game, this one at Port of Spain had a reputation for getting slower and easier as a match wore on. These two factors, and the additional psychological one of exposing the England batsmen immediately to pressure, without allowing them the chance to get used to the atmosphere in the field, were the reasons for Kanhai's decision to put England in. Nevertheless, though events proved his reasoning triumphantly correct it was a brave decision. To ask the other side to bat first after winning a Test Match toss is *always* a gamble. Nothing is so galling than to see the opposition then get away to a good start.

29

And never is criticism so freely bandied about than when this gamble is taken and fails. Indeed, although wrongly quoted in the West Indies as saying that he would have put the opposition in, Mike Denness was in fact honest enough to admit to me that he would have chosen to bat if he had won the toss.

Today, though, Kanhai had to wait only fifteen minutes for justification. Keith Boyce, that magnificent athlete and whole-hearted cricketer, was unleashed first from the northern end like a greyhound from a trap. In his first over Boycott received a magnificent bouncer, pitching only a little short of a length and flying past his nose at alarming speed. Even to have attempted to hook such a ball would have been suicide – probably literal suicide. His cap was dislodged as he flung back his head to get out of line and although he replaced it with apparently unruffled dignity, the gauntlet was already down. Boyce had shown at once that there was moisture enough in the pitch for the ball to rear uncomfortably. In such circumstances, with bounce likely to be uneven and the ball still hard and new, the hook shot must inevitably have been a dangerous gamble, especially if essayed by a batsman who was not well set.

But since Dennis Lillee in 1972 had induced the first serious doubts about Boycott's ability to conquer really top-class fast bowling, he had become a compulsive hooker. Normally Boycott, as an ultra-professional professional, approaches his batting as a businessman approaches a deal. He will take on only what it is going to pay him to take on. Shots likely to get him out will be eliminated until they are perfected in the nets – and then used only when the time is right. But with Boycott the hook had become a matter of pride. The more people said that he should not play it, the more determined he was to prove to everyone that he could. Time and again, uppish hooks from his bat had been swallowed up at fine-leg by fielders unable to believe that a great batsman would hand them his wicket in this way. The compulsion to hook was easily the greatest flaw in Boycott's technique. He must have known it. Certainly the bowlers and Kanhai knew it. So when the captain put Bernard Julien at long-leg even he could not have *expected* Boycott to sell his wicket there as cheaply as he had done in England.

In the first tense quarter of an hour, Boyce and Julien kept the ball mainly up to the bat. Neither batsman looked comfortable, but they could hardly have been expected to do so at such an early stage in the innings. Boycott made the first six runs of the England total. And then Boyce bowled short again. It was on the off stump, even a little outside it, and I am not certain that it was even intended to be the bouncer or the ball which invited the hook. Yet Boycott, more like a schoolboy than a master batsman, got hurriedly into position – some sort of position but not far enough across to ensure that he could turn his wrists as he played the shot and keep the ball down. Inevitably the ball soared high up off the top edge and for a few perspiring moments that cacophonous crowd of 25,000 was silent and still as the lithe figure of Bernard Julien circled beneath the downfalling ball. As he plucked it out of the sky in front of his chest the spectators leapt and roared in delight and disbelief, whilst the few Englishmen amongst them groaned in anguish, fearing what might follow.

Sure enough, England never recovered from the shock of such a start.

Dennis Amiss had begun the tour with scores of 114, 28, 109, 34 and 86, and he would gladly have traded half those runs for even fifty now. But the pressure-cooker atmosphere seemed to bear down particularly heavily on him. He pushed and tucked for six runs and then, when Gary Sobers took over from Keith Boyce at the northern end, he tried half-heartedly to cut at the very first ball, a sharply rising delivery which would have been best left alone, and Murray was presented with a simple catch.

Amiss had faced just 27 balls (twelve more than Boycott) and lasted for over half an hour in company with Mike Denness, who was truly receiving a baptism of fire in his first full Test as captain. Denness did well in the trying circumstances, but Kanhai and his team, with first blood drawn, were not to be denied. The left-armed Bernard Julien had already shown an ability not only to fire the ball away towards the slips across the batsman's body from an awkward angle, but also occasionally to bring the ball back sharply from the off. Denness had made nine when he received one of those late inswingers, a vicious ball which also kept unpleasantly low. Back went his middle stump. 23 for 3, and Denness out to an almost unplayable ball: he was one of the few batsmen who could claim later that he had not contributed to his own downfall.

Keith Fletcher, that introverted enigma of a cricketer, lasted only fourteen balls, during the course of which he achieved a controlled edge through the slips for four off Sobers, before he too was bowled by a Julien inswinger. A superb ball, certainly, with the lateness of the swing deceiving the batsman. But Fletcher had been aiming to drive through the covers: a stroke too ambitious for a player so new to the crease.

Thirty for 4, and no release now, it seemed, from the intense pressure — pressure of weather, of a babbling, roaring crowd, of testing swing bowling and vulture-like fieldsmen. But Frank Hayes has a calm head and a sound technique, and Tony Greig is a man who refuses to be dominated by anyone or anything. Eventually the seamers had to be rested and for once it was a relief to see the sinewy figure of Lance Gibbs present his sun-hat to the umpire and commence a brief spell of teasingly floated off-spinners.

At the other end, little Inshan Ali, looking like a

schoolboy amongst the celebrities around him, served
Greig with two full-tosses, and for this one over in the day
an England player took the attack to the enemy. He swung
the first into the crowd at mid-wicket – the Carib Beer
stand where the cheap seats are and where thousands were
packed together, mostly clad in yellow eyeshades freely
donated by a local firm. Another full-toss hopped first
bounce against the tall wire-meshed fence in front of the
same mid-wicket boundary. Ten runs in the over: riches
indeed on this morning of struggle and scarcity!

At lunch Greig and Hayes were still together, England
were 71 for 4, and talk of them being bowled out for
fewer than their lowest-ever score against the West
Indies – 103 – seemed mercifully premature. Hayes had
batted perhaps best of all, with his ability to wait until the
last moment to play his strokes. He had made only twelve
but only once had he been beaten in seventy minutes of
watchful defence.

So the afternoon began with Kanhai's bold gesture
already vindicated, but with English hopes high that
something might yet be salvaged from the wreckage. But
anyone who lingered a moment too long over his lunchtime Rum and Coke missed the beginning of the end. Gary
Sobers had led the fielders out after lunch and by the time
his colleagues had arrived was practising his graceful run-up
for his first bowl from the pavilion end. As he had
dismissed Amiss with his very first ball, so he now
dismissed Frank Hayes. This time it was an innocuous-
looking ball of full length on the off stump. Hayes played
lazily at it and the ball skidded off at comfortable height
to Roy Fredericks in the gully. 71 for 5.

Alan Knott began surprisingly well considering his poor
form, but, with Boyce freshened by his prandial rest and
now unleashed with redoubled fury, this pitch, despite its
reputation for sluggishness, suddenly seemed possessed of
devils. Although a couple of sharp showers in the

afternoon injected new life into it, the devils were mainly in the batsmen's minds – but that was enough. Knott pushed defensively without conviction, and two of his stumps were uprooted, while Greig flicked at a rapid half-volley down the leg side and Deryck Murray excelled himself by taking off to hold a brilliant catch. Next, Boyce ripped through Pat Pocock's defences, and then, just as 'Chilly' Old (C.Old) seemed to be ordering a temporary halt to the triumphal West Indian march, Kanhai brought on Inshan Ali again and Old holed out to his very first ball – a long hop.

It was that sort of day, when for one side everything went right and for the other, nothing. Despite a last-wicket stand of 15 by Underwood and Willis, using up three-quarters of an hour which might better have been spent in the field, England were all out for 131. Boyce had taken 4 for 42, Julien 2 for 14 and Sobers 2 for 37.

Nor was there to be any consolation for England that night, though Willis and Old did all they could to break through. Willis, in the absence of Snow, had become first-choice fast bowler and he had no compunction about frequently banging the ball in short. Fredericks, badly out of form and having twice fallen cheaply for the President's XI against MCC, was clearly disconcerted and before a single run had been scored he pushed the simplest of gully catches to Mike Denness, guiding the ball gently towards him like a man giving catching practice to a team-mate. But poor Denness, no doubt with a hundred things on his mind, suddenly lunged at the ball just as he seemed to have grasped it. To add insult to grievous injury, Fredericks flashed again at the next rising ball from Willis and it flew over the top of the slips for four. But Rowe at the other end looked immediately impressive, turning one ball late off his legs for four with exquisite timing. In any case, any further chance for England to embarrass the West Indies was lost when another heavy shower ended a triumphant

Opening shots: Geoff Boycott loses his cap to one of Keith
Boyce's bouncers in the first minutes of the first Test. Soon
afterwards he hooked another short ball from the same
bowler—with fatal results.

Left The cares of captaincy: neither Denness nor Kanhai had successful series with the bat, and both were given an uncomfortable foretaste of things to come in the first innings of the first Test. *Above* Denness loses his middle stump to Julien, to the leaping delight of his opposite number. *Below* It is Alan Knott's turn to raise his arms as Pocock bowls Kanhai through the gate.

Above right The menace and determination of Keith Boyce (first Test). Umpire Sang Hue scrutinises the crease; with the exception of Sobers, all the faster bowlers of both sides had difficulty with the front-foot rule. *Below* Tony Greig replies—in his 'old' style.

The famous run-out that never was, at the close of the second day of the first Test. *From top to bottom* Julien plays defensively forward to the last ball of the day from Underwood. Greig, at close silly-point, misfields; then, with his back to the wicket-keeper Knott, who has taken up the stumps at the striker's end, he throws down the non-striker's wicket, with Kallicharran already on his way to the pavilion. Umpire Sang Hue raises his finger. The ITN film shows that the batsman had never touched his bat down after backing up and suggests something of the confusion in the minds of the other England fielders. The appeal was later withdrawn by England after a tense two-and-a-half-hour meeting.

opening day for the West Indies.

I was surprised that night in the hotel by the equanimity of the England team. Relaxed and smiling, you would have thought they had just scored 300 for 4. 'There's no point in getting depressed,' said Donald Carr. 'It can only get better,' said Dennis Amiss. To a professional cricketer it was just another day.

The second day of the match was destined to have surely the most momentous ending to a day's Test cricket on any ground at any time. But even before the notorious 'run-out that never was', the cricket was such that it was a day to be remembered, with England regaining much of the ground which they had lost (or, to a large extent, given away) on the opening day, only to lose most of it again in the final session.

Having dropped Fredericks before he had scored, England quickly rectified matters on the second morning before an excited capacity crowd of 30,000. The little Guyanese left-hander was very well caught by Alan Knott off the top edge as he tried to hook a sharply rising ball from Chris Old.

Lawrence Rowe made 13 and was there long enough to suggest that he was a player of the highest class, but Willis produced a fine ball to dismiss him, which moved late off the seam. Rowe sparred at it and Knott took one of his very best catches, right-handed, low and falling forwards. Rowe could hardly drag himself away. This, though, was to be the high point of the match for Knott, who, perhaps understandably, looked much less brilliant keeping up to the spinners on a pitch where the bounce became increasingly variable.

Kallicharran had come in at number three and began confidently enough, and at 27 for 2 Clive Lloyd loped out to join him. With Frank Hayes crossing from long leg to long leg at either end and both bowlers banging the ball in short, the tactics were obvious. Sure enough, both Lloyd and 'Kalli' essayed dangerous-looking hooks, but when Lloyd got hold of the shot at last the ball flew high into the crowd at fine leg. Delirium, of course, but the first taste of wine went to Lloyd's head. Next ball, he aimed a flourishing drive outside the off stump and – wonder of wonders – it was Mike Denness in the gully who took a good, fast catch, far harder than the one he had spilled on the previous evening. 63 for 3; two wickets to Old and an impressive start by England, especially by the Yorkshire fast bowler, who in this one spell, despite several no-balls, found an easy rhythm and an extra yard of pace. He now gave Rohan Kanhai a torrid time, and the West Indian captain, unsettled and strangely injudicious for one of such ripe experience, was lucky to survive as long as he did.

While the captain struggled, however, Kallicharran began to sparkle. He had looked confident and assured from the start and with three successive fours off Greig he brought up the hundred. Kanhai had made only eight of a partnership of 43 when he pushed out at Pocock and was bowled through the gate. Kallicharran again restored the balance by reaching a spirited fifty in 107 minutes with five fours and at lunch West Indies were 112 for 4, straining uncertainly to make good their advantage.

The quick bowlers had forced England back into the match, and the spinners were to keep them there for much of the afternoon. Garfield Sobers was lazily comfortable, Kallicharran admirably patient, but for a long time the going was slow and stern. It was a special triumph for Derek Underwood to get Sobers out for 23, caught at wide mid-on as he drove without getting to the pitch of the ball, because Sobers in his time had handed out a lot of punishment to the Kent left-hander, who had never previously taken his wicket in a first-class match.

Still England made progress through the long West Indies order, though Kallicharran remained, more dangerous the longer he stayed. Murray, fortunate when he hit Underwood perilously close to Boycott at mid-on, played a useful innings of 19 in a stand of 49 before, soon after tea, he top-edged a sweep at Pocock and Fletcher took a simple catch at slip.

Now came the crucial period of the day. With West Indies 196 for 6 there was still a chance that England might keep their lead within reasonable bounds, but, as has happened in many a Test, the taking of the new ball was to prove a godsend to the batsmen. At this stage, too, the weather took a hand again. Rain held up play for twenty minutes when Kallicharran was 95 not out, but as soon as play resumed he pulled Underwood firmly for four. Three of the crowd thought that it was going to be a six and unable to stop themselves ran onto the field for a premature celebration. No sooner had they arrived in the middle than three giant-striding policemen in white helmets came bearing down upon them, and the crowd was treated to a hilarious sprinting chase, with all three of the pursued being hauled to safety just in time over the ten-foot-high wire fences which guard the boundary.

No sooner had they clambered over than 'Kalli' leant back and pulled another four to bring up his third Test hundred in 264 minutes with ten fours. The next three-quarters of an hour's cricket produced a further 60 runs. Willis and Old, so penetrating in the morning and armed now with a bright new ball, were helpless against the flashing sabre that was Kallicharran's bat. Twice before, he had reached three figures in a Test and then quickly succumbed. Now he took outrageous chances again, but this time he hit so hard that even his edged strokes went for four. For a time England did not know where to bowl at him, and Julien at the other end was – for a player of such limited experience – marvellously restrained. In a game much closer than the winning margin of seven wickets suggests, this stand of exactly one hundred between Kallicharran and Julien was the most important of all. It was interrupted by the notorious run-out at the close of this second day, an event of such importance that it will be discussed separately in the next chapter.

Suffice to say here that, due to diplomacy and not a little good fortune, the hullaballoo had virtually died out when play began again on the Tuesday following the rest day. It was a beautiful sunny morning and the goodwill everyone felt was symbolised publicly when Tony Greig and Alvin Kallicharran extended hands of friendship to one another in the middle of the pitch.

Kallicharran added a further 16 runs but was not the same player on the third day, three times being dropped off Pat Pocock – once by Knott at the wicket and twice by Amiss at leg-slip – before finally lofting the deserving Surrey off-spinner to Underwood at mid-on. His great innings of 158 was over, his runs scored out of a total of 296.

Now the greatest difference between the two sides was severely underlined: Julien and Boyce at numbers eight and nine in the batting order compared with Old and Pocock for England. On this occasion Boyce lasted a mere ten balls and nine minutes during the space of which he hit the ball with such primeval violence that he scored 26 runs with two sixes and three fours. Another huge crowd danced in ecstasy.

Julien had played second fiddle in two stands but now it was the turn of this immensely talented all-rounder to lead the orchestra himself. Tunefully he did so, hitting the ball with effortless good timing through the covers and off his legs. His fifty, scored in 151 minutes, contained eight fours and he was 86 not out when the innings closed neatly just before lunch at 392 – a massive first-innings lead of 261. Julien thus narrowly missed a hundred in successive Tests, while for England Pat Pocock took 5 for 110 in 43 overs.

His bowling had been the one big plus in the English performance in the field. Denness had not always looked in control of the situation and it was disconcerting to see his Kent colleagues Knott and Underwood from time to time offering what appeared to be unsolicited advice. If, from this point of view, the authoritative captaincy of Illingworth (watching the match from the Press box) had been missed, it was good to see the new England off-spinner really trying to give the ball a tweak on a pitch which encouraged and rewarded genuine spin. As a bowler Illingworth had always been a skilful user of the air, but rarely an energetic tweaker. His presence in the side ahead of Pocock since 1968 had been thoroughly justified, but it had held back the latter's progress since his promising Caribbean tour under Cowdrey earlier that year.

England began the long hot afternoon knowing that they must double their first-innings score even to make the West Indies bat again. It is amazing what sunshine on a batsman's back can do, and there was a much greater impression of comfort at the crease as Boycott and Amiss went about their critical duties with admirable calm and devotion to duty. If anything, Amiss was the more assured of the two early on, with Boycott, his mind at last made up that the hook must remain a forbidden weapon in his armoury, at times uncertain exactly what to do when a short ball came along. Both openers were struck on the pads by the ball coming back which both Sobers and Julien bowl so well, but there were mercifully few alarms.

Boyce was allowed only three subdued overs with the new ball and by the eleventh over of the innings the familiar figure of Lance Gibbs was wheeling away with his usual accuracy and skilfully varied flight, his first spell of 21 overs costing only 21 runs. Inshan Ali was accurate enough too, but the little man's turn was slow, his flight lacking in subtlety. Several times Boycott, not the most fleet-footed of players, was able to come down the pitch to hit him on the full-toss to the mid-wicket boundary. At tea, England were 96 without loss and amongst their supporters a small bubble of hope was slowly growing, a bubble which was not to burst until after lunch on the following day.

Boycott and Amiss reached their fifties within a few minutes of each other, Boycott with eight fours, Amiss with five. Some brilliant fielding kept them in check but never inactive as they batted serenely through the afternoon, reaching the 200-mark in 237 minutes and passing the previous highest England partnership for the first wicket in the West Indies. Amiss had one brief uncomfortable period against Lance Gibbs, but by the close England were 201 for no wicket, the deficit was only 60 and the game was very much alive again.

Never was the glorious unpredictability of cricket so dramatically displayed as on the fourth day of this first Test Match. The English team on the previous evening had been quietly confident that they could now save the game and, as one of them said at the time, 'that would be a damned good effort after our first-innings display'. When soon after lunch they reached 326 for 1, it seemed inconceivable that an even worse display of batting should throw the match away, or that, by the end of the day, West Indies should be a mere 55 runs away from victory.

Rohan Kanhai decided not to take the new ball in the morning, though everyone had expected him to do so. It is a sign of a confident captain when the obvious move is not necessarily made, and Kanhai was proved right because the much-prized wicket of Boycott was taken when only eight runs had been added to the overnight total. Boycott had reached 93 when he pushed out at Lance Gibbs and Fredericks at forward short-leg took a good low catch off the inside edge. 209 was just three runs short of Reg Simpson and Cyril Washbrook's highest-ever opening partnership against West Indies, scored at Trent Bridge in 1950 when the circumstances which followed were remarkably similar to those at Port of Spain twenty-three years later.

At Nottingham the fatal England collapse had been started by a run-out. The same thing was to happen here, though this time England did not immediately fold after the departure of Boycott. Indeed Dennis Amiss started to play better than ever and with Mike Denness he added a further 119 runs. The captain must have been desperately close to being out l.b.w. to Gibbs soon after coming in (the umpire ruling in his favour being Ralph Gosein, who had come in for some unjustified criticism from one journalist) and was also missed early on by Rowe at slip – a difficult chance. But the advent of the new ball when the score was 239 helped him to settle, whilst Amiss greeted it with almost as much gusto as had Kallicharran. He scored particularly freely in the square-leg region with several of the beautifully timed flicks off his legs which are his speciality. His concentration and positive attitude in this innings were beyond reproach. He reached 150 with one of several well-taken quick singles, having batted 340 minutes and hit 18 fours, and nine runs later passed his highest Test score made the previous winter against Pakistan in Hyderabad. Denness kept him gradually more certain company, playing some good straight and on-drives, though like so many of England's leading players of the present time he declined too many invitations to hit the ball through extra-cover.

At lunch England were 315 for 1. I did a broadcast at the time and was asked whether I thought the match was saved. 'Yes,' I said, and even suggested that if the England progress continued it was not out of the question that they might score enough runs to give the West Indies an embarrassing final day on a turning wicket. But a certain native caution, reinforced by having seen so many England collapses in the last few years, made me add: 'But of course England are not yet out of the woods altogether.'

Rarely has pessimism been more justified by events. At 326, Amiss leant back and forced a ball away past cover. Twinkle-footed Kallicharran set off towards the boundary in pursuit. To some fielders the shot was worth three runs, but not to 'Kalli'. He had the ball in his hand as the batsmen set off without conviction for the third run. The return was as swift and low as the flight of a swallow. Denness out for 44. England 328 for 2.

Gary Sobers has hammered more nails into more England coffins than anyone since Bradman. This afternoon the emperor of all-round cricketers felt like a bowl. It was a bit hot for his quicker stuff, so, since bowling of any kind to Sobers is second nature, he decided to try a little spell of orthodox left-arm spin. Walking one pace into his delivery stride, he achieved all that was necessary with absurd ease: perfect length, excellent direction, a trajectory difficult to attack, and considerable turn off the pitch. Amiss was l.b.w. padding up to the ball which came on with the arm. Umpire Gosein had no doubts, and if others did England could not complain. Nonetheless, it was a disappointing end to a great innings of 174 made in over six and a half hours.

Keith Fletcher, almost suffocated by close fielders, lasted three balls, tried to drive without getting to the pitch, and edged to Rowe at slip, who made no mistake. Gerry Gomez commented: 'If you had played that shot as a schoolboy, you would certainly have expected an angry word about it afterwards from your captain.' 338 for 4, and a mere eleven runs later Hayes tried to pull Sobers, another hazardous shot on a wicket where the bounce was becoming increasingly variable. The ball kept low and came off the under-edge onto his stumps.

The situation cried out now for determination and a grim backs-against-the-wall resistance. If Ken Barrington, Trevor Bailey, Bev Congdon, Slasher Mackay, or any of cricket's renowned fighters had been faced with this situation they would have stuck to the wickets like leeches. Yet Greig and Knott, England's last serious line of defence, played more like lemmings, stepping away to cut against Lance Gibbs's sharp spin as if they had never heard of the dangers of cutting an off-spinner. Of course they were not *trying* to get out. But it was as if they had lost all discipline, all tactical awareness, all knowledge of technical basics, all sense of how much was at stake, all feelings of shame at knocking down in the space of minutes a defensive wall which Amiss and Boycott had taken hours to build.

Gibbs, like Sobers impervious to the passing years, and with the scent of victory in his nostrils, gave nothing away. Greig pushed forward and was bowled; Knott cut and was caught at slip; Old drove and was caught by the bowler; Pocock got the merest tickle and walked before anyone could think of appealing; Underwood mowed to mid-wicket. These last five wickets all fell to Gibbs, brushed away like so many irritating flies.

Again the West Indies deserved the credit for refusing to release the initiative once they had regained it. But if for an Englishman it was humiliating to watch, imagine the shame and remorse in the tourists' dressing-room when the full agony of what had happened began to sink in! Eight wickets had fallen for 64 runs in under two hours.

It would have needed super-resilience to have recovered from the horror of the afternoon's events quickly enough to turn back the game again. West Indies had only 132 to make to record their first Test win in the Caribbean for nine years and their first over England on home ground for two decades. By the time England had come out of their state of trauma and West Indies had started to think of the significance of their victory and become a little frightened by the prospect, it was too late. Rowe failed again, but Fredericks set off in pursuit of the total like a racehorse from the stalls and by the close of the day only 55 more runs were needed.

The final morning mocked England by giving them a tantalising glimpse of what might have been. In the second over Kallicharran hit Underwood straight to Greig at mid-wicket (and, incidentally, waited to be given out as if he now had a double life in every innings) and then in the same over Lloyd gave Frank Hayes his second short-leg catch. At first Kanhai reacted to the crisis like an inexperienced colt, but unlike the English players he was not punished for his folly. Another 100 runs would have made the finish fatal to the fingernails, but there were just too few runs for England to play with and some loose leg-side balls from Pocock were enough to set Kanhai on his merry way with several monumental leg-side swings. Fredericks at the other end never looked troubled and with six to win Denness conceded victory by giving the ball to Fletcher. Kanhai responded with a back-handed sweep for four past third man.

The last rites were played out amidst a continual din of whistles and horns and the clanging of impromptu steel bands as some seven thousand Trinidadians, who had paid to see just an hour of play, celebrated in their own gloriously uninhibited way. Carnival was not due officially for another three weeks; but this was Carnival time already. Even a torrential downpour twenty minutes after the end of the match could not quench the ardour of their joyful dancing. But for the English team, watching the puddles grow within minutes on the outfield, this was the final irony.

4

The Run-Out That Never Was

Even given the advantage of writing some time after the event, it is difficult to assess the true significance of the incidents which occurred immediately after the last ball of the second day of the first Test Match which, for a few hours, threatened to ruin the whole tour. The film of what happened was shown *ad nauseam* at the time in both England and the West Indies, but details are quickly forgotten so it is perhaps worth recalling them briefly here.

The two not-out West Indies batsmen, Bernard Julien and Alvin Kallicharran, had for some time been watching the clock as it moved towards close of play at 5.30, and it was clearly apparent that they had lost interest in scoring runs, their sole intention being to preserve their wickets and so to start afresh on the third day. Both batsmen, most of the crowd and all of the fielders knew well that when Derek Underwood moved in to bowl the sixth ball of his over to Julien, it was the last ball of the day. Julien played a forward defensive stroke past Tony Greig, who was fielding very close at silly point. As Greig ran after the ball with his back to the striker's end, Alan Knott, as is his regular habit, picked off the bails and uprooted the stumps. Meanwhile, at the non-striker's end, Kallicharran had hesitated only a moment having backed up some three yards and then, without returning to his crease, walked on towards the pavilion. Greig by now had collected the ball. He ran on a yard or so, took aim and hurled down the non-striker's wicket. Throwing his arms in the air he appealed and Umpire Sang Hue, who had not yet called 'time' for the day, had no option but to give the batsman out. For a moment the spectators, who had been preparing themselves to welcome home the batting hero of the day, were stunned. Greig clapped his hands and marched briskly in to the pavilion, where the crescendo of indignant booing quickly indicated to him the enormity of his action.

One's immediate reaction was to conclude that something wrong had been done. Kallicharran had defied all that the England bowlers had produced since early in the day and to get him out in this way seemed somehow cheap and dishonourable. Certainly the batsman had been technically wrong in walking to the pavilion without waiting for the umpire's official signal. Certainly, too, Greig was within his rights to punish Kallicharran for his indiscretion. But the fact that – unknown to Greig – Knott had taken out the stumps at the other end equally certainly made the dismissal morally wrong.

In the West Indies many of the crowd carry transistor radios and often have the commentary turned up so loudly that the umpires have to signal to the commentary box to request that the culprits be asked to turn down the volume lest the noise disturb the players. It may well be that the commentary had a significant effect on what happened next. Gerry Gomez, who had been describing the final over's play, gave a very fair summary of what had happened and asked for an opinion from the comments man, the former Trinidad batsman Alvin Corneil. The latter, reasonably enough, set great store by the fact that Alan Knott had removed the stumps – a fact which *appeared* to put Greig in a very bad light. I, meanwhile, had seen Mike Denness speaking to umpire Sang Hue as he left the field and suggested that Denness might have been asking for the appeal to be withdrawn. I also said that I thought Greig had not been able to see Knott when he threw down the wicket at the other end.

It transpired that I was correct in the latter opinion but incorrect in surmising that Denness was at this stage considering withdrawing the appeal, for he had no real power to do so. The captain had merely inquired of the umpire whether he had called 'time' or 'over', to which the answer was obviously 'no'. However the suggestion did in the end turn out to be an inspired guess and in any case it may have helped to persuade the men operating the scoreboard to change back the number of wickets from seven to six. It was this action, more than anything else, which prevented a really serious demonstration, because the vast majority of the 30,000 crowd went home believing that Kallicharran would be reinstated.

In truth, it took a meeting of two and a half hours' duration to find a way out of the problem. Many people wrote later that the decision should not have been changed, that to do so was tampering with inviolate laws. In fact there was a precedent for an umpire's decision being reversed — when Cyril Washbrook was recalled after being given out l.b.w. at Christchurch in 1951, following words between the umpire and the New Zealand captain, Walter Hadlee. (Other half-precedents are recorded at the end of the book.)

As for suggestions that to change the decision was giving way to 'mob rule', only those present could have appreciated the awful feeling one had that if peace had not been quickly restored the tour would have gone ahead in a miserable atmosphere of bitterness. With relationships between the teams impaired there would inevitably have been more incidents and consequently more trouble with the crowds. The game would have become a war and, as such, not worth playing.

During the momentous meeting the tension in the pavilion was incredible as Donald Carr, officials of the West Indian Board of Control, the umpires and the captains discussed the position. Outside, police patrolled in case of trouble: already they had put out one fire in a stand at the far end of the ground. The issues were discussed heatedly. One elderly legal gentleman, well-lubricated with alcohol, went about condemning apartheid in the foullest imaginable language. Others discussed whether there had ever been a precedent for an umpire's decision being overruled or an appeal withdrawn. One remembered Jackie McGlew of South Africa being run out after colliding with a fielder and Colin Cowdrey unsuccessfully attempting to have his innings restored, but not until afterwards was the Washbrook precedent recalled.

The players, meanwhile, had begun to speak to one another again. The story went that Kallicharran had broken his bat on the dressing-room floor in his initial fury. But eventually the traditional close of play beer was shared by the teams. It is ironic that Gary Sobers, who had been the first to forgive Greig and to understand that what he had done had borne no malicious intent, was later quoted as saying that he thought Greig should go home. It was Sobers who shepherded Greig out of the pavilion and drove him back to his hotel. 'He'll be safe in the same car as Gary,' they said.

If this sounds melodramatic, it is no more than the truth. Cricket means so much in the West Indies. Revenge might well have been sought, and Greig, six foot seven and a half inches tall, could not easily disguise himself with glasses and a false beard. But though fear of reprisals or possible crowd disturbances was one good reason for the decision to be changed, it was not the main one. The most important reason was that, perhaps unintentionally, an injustice had been done: an injustice not within the laws of the game, but most definitely within its spirit. Cricket would not be cricket if it were played solely according to the book of laws.

While Greig was being given safe conduct the cricketers of both sides, and Kallicharran in particular, were all smiles again. Goodwill was in the air. Somehow a solution would be found. The rumour was, though, that umpire Douglas

Sang Hue was being stubborn. 'You must not undermine my authority,' he demanded. An admirable man, Sang Hue: afraid of no one, much more than a mere official in a white coat. In the end, he *was* overruled, but certainly not undermined. He gained in stature.

At last, soon after eight o'clock, the word filtered through the hot, dark pavilion that a decision had been reached. There was a rush for the Press box, where a statement was to be made which might make or break a tour which was still in its infancy. Donald Carr looked tense, drawing hungrily at a cigarette. Jeffrey Stollmeyer, tall, urbane, distinguished-looking, was relaxed and smiling. It was he who read the statement:

'Under the laws of cricket, the batsman, Kallicharran, was run out and the umpire had no option but to give the decision which he made.

The West Indies captain, Rohan Kanhai, has expressed complete satisfaction that the decision was correct and the only one to be given under the circumstances.

Whilst appreciating that this is not strictly within the laws of cricket, England's manager, Donald Carr, and captain, Mike Denness, have in the interests of cricket as a whole and the future of this tour in particular, requested that the appeal against the batsman be withdrawn. The umpires, bearing in mind the particular circumstances, have agreed to accept this request and Kallicharran will therefore continue his innings.

The England player concerned, Tony Greig, in no way intended his instinctive action to be contrary to the spirit of the game and he is truly sorry that this has caused an unhappy situation.

Both captains have expressed the view that this incident will in no way affect the amicable relationships which exist between the two teams.

These decisions were taken with the approval and support of the West Indies Cricket Board of Control, present at the match.'

They were surely the right decisions. Indeed the statement was a masterpiece of diplomacy, from which no one lost face, not even Tony Greig.

Greig himself, of course, now became the centre of attention. Had his action been sharp practice? Would he have to be sent home? Would he lose his position as vice-captain? All these questions were freely discussed at the time, but Greig swam free from the deep water with remarkable speed and resilience, and, in the end, was at least partially exonerated.

Greig's special responsibility as a South African-born person and as vice-captain has already been mentioned. He is well-known as a stern competitor who will give nothing away as a cricketer and who hates to lose. Yet, ironically, he had already won considerable popularity amongst the West Indian crowds. They loved the way he stood with his bat not touching the ground, the way he walked in like a giraffe if he were fielding on the boundary or crouched down almost in the batsman's pocket when he was fielding at silly-point. In the very over before he so pragmatically and ruthlessly threw down Kallicharran's wicket, he had been stretching out a telescopic arm to pat the little man on the head to a roar of laughter from the crowd. Yet in an instant the clown became the villain.

But was he a villain? In my view (and in the final analysis the matter must be one of personal opinion) he committed no great crime, and certainly a crime no worse than many that had been perpetrated in Test cricket before – one thinks of English bodyline tactics in 1932, of Australian administrators who condoned in the late 1950s and early 1960s what was widely considered to be illegal bowling, of the West Indian fast bowler Charlie Griffith running out a batsman backing up without prior warning, of South African players who hit the ball but would not walk, of Oriental cricketers who have taken similar advantage of weak umpiring. In other words, no country is better than any other in this respect. From time to time in Test cricket there have always been incidents which have left a nasty taste in the mouth.

Nevertheless, though Greig was within his rights and though the fact that he had not been in a position to see Knott removing the stumps cleared him of any charge of sharp practice, his action was ungracious. It was not worthy of an admirable cricketer, or of someone who, off the field, is a charming personality. Certainly Greig himself learned a painful lesson from what happened.

That the situation did not turn out to be more serious was due to the diplomacy of the officials concerned and also to good fortune. I have already said that the changing of the scoreboard prevented serious demonstrations amongst the crowd. As I came out of the commentary box, for instance, one angry man bellowed up to me, brandishing his fist, 'Is he out?' 'I'm not sure,' I replied, 'but I think the appeal will be withdrawn.' 'You are lucky' was his reply. There is no friendlier Caribbean crowd than the one at Port of Spain, generally speaking, but had the decision not been changed there would surely have been trouble; nor would the other West Indian countries quickly have forgotten what had happened. In the end sixteen runs was the price for the quelling of many bitter reproaches and the avoidance of a miserable tour.

It was fortunate too that Donald Carr, the manager, had, as Secretary of the TCCB, the power to take a top-level decision on the spot. Had it been necessary for calls to be made to Lord's on a Sunday evening, the situation would have been further complicated and the problem much less quickly resolved. Again, it was lucky that the rest day should have followed, giving time for tempers to cool. Finally, a rift between the teams was avoided not least because, with all but one of the West Indian team involved in county cricket in England, this was a series between friendly rivals who spoke the same kind of language. It did not lessen the rivalry, but it meant that there was a greater chance for matches to be chivalrously conducted.

It is probably true that had a West Indian run out, say, Geoff Boycott, as Greig had run out Kallicharran, or had the incident happened instead in England, where passions are cooler, the decision would not have been changed. But that does not alter my opinion that at that particular time and in that particular place, the right decision was taken.

5

Sabina Park — A Batsman's Haven

Touching down in Kingston, Jamaica, along the pencil-thin runway of Palisadoes Airport, with blue sea on every side, you might at first think you were arriving in just another Caribbean island. But once you have driven round the slim promontory of land and on into the capital itself, you feel as though you have entered a large international city. Peeling paint, tumbledown walls and the ragged, surly look of the inhabitants in the poorer areas of this city, where twenty-five per cent are unemployed and a staggering forty per cent are under fourteen years old — all are symptoms of a place with a phenomenal crime rate. In the toughest areas of the city someone is shot almost every day and guns are exchanged on the black market for marijuana grown in Jamaica itself. When the MCC were there the Government under its able and idealistic young Prime Minister, Michael Manley, was also grappling with a commodity shortage which included not just fuel but also staple Jamaican products such as sugar and rice.

But this is only one face of Kingston. There are proud new buildings too and intercontinental hotels which look across to the barren blue mountains in the distance, mountains more massive in appearance than the more intimate jungle-coated hills behind Port of Spain.

Sabina Park itself, where large modern stands are now under construction which will transform the ground, was, before work on the project commenced, a strange mixture of the shabby and the idyllic — a contrast which indeed applies to Jamaica itself. At the north end of the ground a twenty-foot-high eau-de-Nile coloured concrete wall was bordered on one side by an ancient three-tiered stand and on the other by two rickety structures with corrugated iron roofs which would shame a Fourth Division English football club.

There was a lot of barbed wire about too, and if you imagined that the loudspeakers which hung from the tall, rotting wooden posts at the edges of the stands were searchlights instead, you might also have imagined yourself to be in *Stalagluft V*, with the white-helmeted Kingston policemen, their black trousers emblazoned with a smart broad red stripe, replaced by haughty 'Heil Hitler' Nazis. Frequently a great black John Crow (a cousin of the vulture) glided with lazy menace overhead, as if waiting for tired fielders to collapse and provide him with his next meal.

Yet behind this austere scene the palms and bread-fruit trees fluttered in the delicate breeze, and the rugged Blue Mountain range shimmered handsomely in the distance. The makeshift commentary box at the southern end of the ground may have been small and stuffy but trying to describe cricket in a context as vibrant with noise and colour as this is a very much easier and more pleasurable experience than doing so, say, at Kennington Oval.

The MCC match against Jamaica proved little. MCC were undeniably the better side, but they were unable to turn superiority into a badly needed win because of rain, injuries and, in the end, a lack of inspiration in the field.

I had been led to believe that the pitch at Sabina Park was always placidity itself. But when a wild-looking bowler named Uton Dowe came steaming over the arid turf, silver medallion swinging across his glistening black chest after the manner of Wesley Hall, and hurled the ball at the batsman like a man possessed, you could not call the wicket placid. True, once you had got used to its pace this was a pitch (unlike Port of Spain) on which you could play your strokes with confidence, but when Dowe was in

54

action early in the match both Boycott and Jameson found his speed disconcerting – or so it looked from the boundary. Jameson, in fact, said later that he had not found Dowe especially quick, but when he was given out caught behind it looked suspiciously as though he had been beaten for pace.

Dowe, at any rate, looked a better bowler now than in a Test the previous year when Keith Stackpole had given him a lot of punishment – punishment so fearful in fact that the Jamaicans invented an eleventh commandment: 'Dowe shalt not bowl.' Not only did he take four good English wickets in the only MCC innings but he worried everyone in the English camp by striking Geoff Boycott four times on the arm or body during an innings of 83 (retired hurt).

Boycott, at this stage, was in some difficulty against short-pitched fast bowling. Having decided to rule out the hook, yet being more inclined to get right behind the line of the ball than almost any other player, he frequently found himself in the path of the ball with no stroke to offer: the attacking shot, the hook, was too risky but so, also, was the defensive shot, because a late rise on the ball might result in his having to fend the ball away with a consequent catch to slips or gully. The only alternative was to try to sway out of line at the last moment, but – perhaps as some legacy from having worn glasses rather than contact lenses in the past – Boycott tended to take his eyes off the ball and so to be hit.

Boycott loudly proclaims his attitude to being hit: 'You've got to pick yourself up, grit your teeth and forget about it. That's what F.S. used to tell me . . . . If you're an opening bat you've got to expect getting hit.' F.S., of course, is Fred Trueman, opening bowler, not opening batsman, whose Yorkshire pride and stentorian Yorkshire voice Boycott has himself adopted.

It is remarkable how many times Boycott has been

injured since having his arm broken by a ball from Graham McKenzie in Australia in 1971, and more than one England cricketer has suggested that he sometimes looks upon injuries as an excuse for failing to score as heavily as he should. Yet no one should ever doubt Boycott's courage for, as I have said, it is partly his determination to get behind the line of the ball at all costs that causes his body to be so vulnerable. It was his forearm which was severely bruised just above the wrist against Jamaica, but mercifully an X-ray at a Kingston hospital revealed that there were no bones broken, and he was passed fit to play in the second Test.

It was the formation of England's team for the Sabina Park Test which added interest to a disappointing match with Jamaica. Bob Taylor, the Derbyshire wicket-keeper, was at last given a game after three weeks of touring without one, and he took his chance so well that his omission from the Test was hardly justice. He kept wicket well, as always, but it was his enterprising innings of 65 which, following another batting failure by Alan Knott, really seemed to have demanded a place for him. Of course it was the brittleness of England's batting that was against him, and there was no question that over the years Knott had proved himself the better batsman. But Taylor had never been given a real chance. This, perhaps, was the moment to take a gamble with him.

Taylor took his latest disappointment with typical fortitude and good grace. This friendly, quiet, pipe-smoking man, with prematurely greying hair, is the very personification of the term 'a good tourist'. In the Jamaican match, however, he was a blameless contributor to another 'incident'. In Geoff Arnold's first over the local hero Lawrence Rowe snicked a ball down the leg-side and Taylor, diving to his left, took a brilliant one-handed catch. Rowe, who admitted afterwards that he had been out but who is not a 'walker', was given the benefit of the doubt by umpire Karl Peart. Of course it was understandable for Geoff Arnold to react angrily to this. He had been omitted from the first Test, much to his disappointment; now he was looking for a successful bowl to regain his place. Rowe was the one man he most wanted to get out and here he was, apparently caught down the leg-side in his very first over and before he had scored a run. And this tall, portly umpire was shaking his head under a large plantation-style straw hat.

These were the factors in Arnold's defence. Against him was the statement issued by the Test and County Cricket Board before the start of the tour warning that public expressions of dissent with umpiring decisions would not be tolerated. Arnold expressed *his* dissent in no uncertain terms. He stood in amazement, stalked back angrily, bowled two bouncers which Rowe gleefully despatched to the boundary and then, when Rowe got up to his end, wagged his finger at him and gestured towards the pavilion. Even the crowd, knowing Rowe to be earning a dollar a run, seemed to agree with Arnold that the umpire should have given him out, but in the light of the Board's warning, of the Kanhai/Fagg incident at Edgbaston, and of the Greig/Kallicharran incident at Port of Spain, Arnold was fortunate perhaps that his only punishment was a public reprimand. In fact, though, he had the additional mortification of bowling without distinction during the rest of the match and of again being left out of the England twelve, even though England's intention had always been to play three seamers at Sabina Park. At this stage, 'Oss' was definitely not enjoying his tour.

Lawrence Rowe in contrast was thoroughly enjoying every moment of the MCC visit. Having had his moment of luck, he went on to make 41 and 118 for his country (British readers must realise that his country is Jamaica, not the West Indies), thus continuing a phenomenal run of high scores against touring sides at Sabina Park. In 1972 he had made 227 for Jamaica against the New Zealanders and he had followed this with his famous and unique performance of a century in each innings on his first Test appearance. (His scores were 214 and 100 not out.) The following year he made 149 against the Australians and followed this with a relatively low-scoring Test Match in which his scores were 76 and 4. This sort of batting, however, was Bradmanesque and it is one of cricket's little curiosities that Rowe should have taken so long to score a first-class century *outside* his native ground. One would have thought the pressures on him to do well in Kingston were almost too much to bear, because the crowd not only expected but demanded that its hero should succeed. In this city where there is so much poverty and illiteracy, Rowe is worshipped like a Caesar.

His choice as opener in the West Indies team had apparently closed the last chink in an almost impregnable armour. For the past decade the selectors had found it difficult to decide on a settled opening pair. In Frank Worrell's great team Joey Carew and Easton McMorris used to vie for the place as Conrad Hunte's partner, but neither was very successful. When Hunte retired Roy Fredericks gradually established himself, but until Rowe's arrival no one had settled down as his regular partner. Indeed the partnership between these two in the second Test was the first century opening partnership for West Indies in five years.

Rowe at this stage was making rapid strides towards becoming a complete Test batsman, but his severe ankle injury, suffered against Australia, had held him back for a time and of the two emerging batting stars it was Kallicharran who first reached maturity. But whether hitting the ball off the back foot with graceful power, flicking it off his legs with masterly timing, or occasionally hooking with thrilling ferocity, Rowe already looked a great player in the manner of George Headley and

Everton Weekes.

Another Jamaican to win a Test place at Sabina Park was Arthur Barrett, a leg-spinner with a good high action, who was to give England more trouble than Inshan Ali had done. In the Jamaican match, however, Barrett proved innocuous, as MCC progressed in workmanlike fashion to a total in excess of 400. Apart from Taylor's breezy innings and Boycott's brave but battered affair, the best batting came from Keith Fletcher, who looked much more at home on a pitch which at least had a bit more pace than the one at Queen's Park Oval. Fletcher's hundred certainly impressed the Jamaicans ('class, man, class' was the comment of their wicket-keeper Desmond Lewis) and it was particularly unfortunate that he should have gone down with a gastric illness three days before the Test Match. There was an even bigger scare in the English camp only 48 hours before the Test when Mike Denness retired to bed with a similar complaint (vomiting and a violent headache). Since Tony Greig had not at that stage been passed fit to play, after receiving a nasty bruise on his calf – hit when fielding at his much-discussed suicide position of silly-point – there was even talk for a few hours that Geoff Boycott would find himself captain of England. But the recovery of Denness was quicker than the recovery of Fletcher, and in the end there was only one enforced change to the England side, John Jameson coming in for Fletcher.

As at Port of Spain, so at Kingston, the Test Match atmosphere was unmistakable. The Saturday morning was hot and sunny, with the tall peaks of the Blue Mountains standing out in sharp relief against an azure sky. The crowd, many of them brushing without tickets past harassed gate officials with false claims to be members of the Press, or possessors of relatives holding their tickets inside, soon filled the ground. One man, asked for his pass at the gate, simply shouted 'legal rights' and barged cheerfully through the arms of a dumbstruck ticket inspector. It was an apt reply indeed, for the West Indian spectator feels rather slighted at being asked to pay for the privilege of watching something that is part of his heritage. Those who could not squeeze into the ground somehow found a place to watch by peeping out of the tops of trees or perching on neighbouring roof-tops.

The early arrivals were entertained by a smart and rhythmical military band resplendent in red tunics and trousers marked with bold red stripes. The word soon got round that Fletcher, having arrived at the ground, had been forced to return to his hotel unwell, so Jameson would come in at first wicket down and Denness would drop down to number five. This time there was no doubt that the successful captain would choose to bat first.

Denness was the lucky one on this occasion, though for a while the crowd was fooled because some of the younger members of the groundstaff turned cartwheels of delight as soon as the coin had landed. They seemed to assume that Kanhai would win the toss as of right.

There was particular interest in the pitch, which, with grass cuttings rolled into the surface, looked exactly like a piece of brown ceiling-board. Several hours' play had been lost to rain during the Jamaica match because of totally inadequate tarpaulin covers which had twice leaked to create neat damp lines down the middle of the pitch. This morning there was another patch on the Test wicket, placed on a length at the southern end. But the problem was quickly overcome by the simple expedient of pitching the wicket two yards farther forward, so that the damp patch appeared inside the popping crease.

On this Sabina Park pitch Ray Illingworth recalled that during Peter May's tour of 1959–60 the Middlesex fast bowler Alan Moss had once pitched a bouncer half way down the wicket which had landed full-toss against the concrete sightscreen. Today the very first ball was a bouncer from Boyce which fluttered by Boycott's nose at a friendly pace and was easily taken by Murray at waist-height; it was clear that the relaid turf held no such 'pace like fire'.

In the first hour Boycott and Amiss made 42 from 16 overs, with both players at ease and Boycott especially impressive. But when he had made 28 Boycott was struck by a swift throw from Clive Lloyd and, as he stretched to try to get out of the way, strained a muscle in his groin which constrained him more the longer he batted. This was extremely bad luck on both Boycott and his side, but it was only one reason why England failed to make the most of winning the toss on a pitch which really offered no help at all to the bowlers.

Dennis Amiss was the first of several to get out to a bad ball. When the score had reached 68 he essayed a savage square-cut to a short leg-break from Barrett, and Kanhai, fielding at extra-cover, dived forward to hold the first of many brilliant catches. Jameson, certainly not a man to be overawed by the occasion, began confidently despite being confronted with spin (not his favourite batting diet) and with a now-subdued Boycott took the score to 87 for 1 at lunch.

Spin was the ration after the interval too – teasing, tantalising spin from Gibbs; mixed, thoughtful spin from Barrett; accurate, aggressive, penetrating spin from Sobers. It was Gibbs who got Jameson and this was no surprise to anyone who had seen the old master bamboozling Jameson in the one-day international at the Oval in September. On this occasion Jameson hit one good blow for four over the top of the on-side field, but when he tried the shot again he was fooled by the flight and stranded so far down the pitch that Murray could have stumped him in his sleep.

Now came the crucial period of the day. Receiving little

61

or no help from Boycott, who was unable to make light of his groin injury despite showing his usual grim dedication, Frank Hayes took forty long minutes to get off the mark. During this time he looked in no trouble, stayed admirably unruffled, and hit a number of handsome strokes straight to a deep-set field. Moreover the cover fielding, especially of Lloyd and Julien, was superlative. Progress for England was painfully slow but at least they were showing application, the lack of which had cost them so dearly at Port of Spain. Thus it was all the more galling when Hayes received a long hop from Sobers, opened wide his eyes at receiving a bad ball at last, and pulled it straight to Boyce at square-leg.

No sooner had Denness come in than England were in all too familiar trouble, at 134 for 4, with Boycott walking disconsolately back to the pavilion. Again the batsman was not without slight blame, for Sobers had called Kanhai up to short extra-cover and it was there that the captain took another superb diving catch, inches from the ground.

Denness and Greig now batted with merciful enterprise and Greig played a fine innings in which he hit the ball with reassuring certainty and aggression. Yet, after he had made 45 of a stand of 90 at the rate of a run a minute with his captain, he too pulled a long hop straight down a fielder's throat. His first mistake had been his last, and though both Hayes and himself were to blame for failing to keep the ball down, it was extraordinary how magnetically the ball seemed to fly straight into enemy hands.

Denness went on to reach a most valuable fifty in 121 minutes and, though he played some embarrassingly streaky shots outside the off stump against Boyce, he could point to the scoreboard with more pride than most of his team. All the same, 251 for 5 at the close of play on such a pitch was a disappointing score. We had seen too much of the artisan, too little of the master craftsman, and nothing at all of genius.

The second day, and the morning in particular, was much more entertaining. England's last five wickets produced a further 102 runs and another tightly packed crowd watched the cricket with humour and appreciation. The day began with Sobers bowling chinamen out of the back of his hand — as if to prove that this most versatile of all cricketers had lost none of his tricks. In the event, both Denness and Knott, the Kentish pair on whom all hopes of a big total rested, played him with some relish, and it was only when Boyce returned to the attack that the English batting uncertainties again became apparent. Denness had played some fine shots but against short-pitched fast bowling his first move was away from the line, not towards it, and he paid the penalty when he failed to get over a Boyce bouncer and was caught at short-leg by Fredericks.

Old played his first ball for two and was caught behind off his second from Julien, but Underwood, although living dangerously, made 24 in spirited fashion before, almost inevitably, he was caught in the slips. Sobers was the bowler, and Fredericks the holder of yet another brilliant catch. Much depended now on Alan Knott, and although he played well he could never dominate the bowling. He made 39 before trying to late-cut Barrett's first ball, a short leg-break which Knott snicked into Murray's gloves. Pocock and Willis now added 20 for the last wicket but England were out ten minutes after lunch for 353, nine of their ten wickets having fallen to catches. It was a respectable total, but on such a wicket certainly no more.

One felt then that the West Indies would soon underline the friendliness of the pitch, and this they did, Fredericks and Rowe making 159 with very little trouble before the close. Willis and Old seemed obsessed at first with trying to get the batsmen out mis-hooking, and by bowling a lot of fairly innocuous short stuff they virtually wasted the new ball and their own energies. Pocock and Underwood were soon wheeling away with great accuracy but little venom, and the fields became increasingly defensive. Fredericks reached fifty first, a streaky affair compared with Rowe's masterly fifty which was greeted by tumultuous applause from the Sabina Park crowd. It seemed amazing that this should have been the first century opening partnership for the West Indies since 1969, but so it was, and though Denness, by relying on Pocock, Underwood and Greig to do the bowling, and by following a policy of ruthless containment, kept the run flow to a trickle, neither Fredericks nor Rowe would give an inch. Concentration and discipline, quite as much as natural flair, were responsible for the strong West Indian position after two days, and England's defensive tactics were the subject of intense – and controversial – discussion during the rest day which followed.

Although the famous innings of 262 not out by Dennis Amiss was eventually to be the chief reason for England saving the match, the strangely pedestrian progress of the West Indies on the third day certainly used up much valuable time. Although only four wickets fell England's bowlers had a very good day, restricting West Indies to 275 runs in six hours and a lead of only 81.

It was fine competitive cricket from the start, with a top-class spell of straight fast bowling by Chris Old and some beautiful strokes from Lawrence Rowe. A flashing cover drive took the score past 173 – the previous highest opening partnership by West Indians against England, scored in 1948 by George Carew and Andy Ganteaume (the man who scored 112 in his first Test Match innings and was never again selected to play for the West Indies: useful ammunition for cricket quizzes). Soon afterwards Rowe completed his third Test century and his tenth in first-class cricket, every one of these innings having been played in his native Kingston. Roy Fredericks was less happy and might have been run out when he found himself stranded half way down the pitch but managed to scramble back when the England close fielders seemed too tantalised to react to the opportunity.

The score had reached 206 and Fredericks 94 when the latter tried to pull Old, now operating with the new ball, and inside-edged the ball onto his stumps. Rowe's riposte was a ferocious hook for six off Willis, but the latter had sweet revenge when the batsman shuffled across his stumps and was l.b.w. for 120.

After lunch tight bowling by Underwood and especially by Greig, who for the first time bowled slow medium off-spin off a full run, kept Lloyd and Kallicharran remarkably quiet until Lloyd moved down the wicket and hit Underwood far out of the ground over the concrete sight-screen – a majestic straight six. But Underwood continued to bowl with three close fielders, a notable change and one which certainly seemed to be paying. Greig bowled 14 overs for only 35 runs and it took a long time for two such renowned stroke players as Lloyd and Kallicharran to take control. But they had added a further 112 runs when just before tea Lloyd played across the line of an off-break from John Jameson, who had bowled very well against Jamaica and was now taking his first Test wicket. I felt sorry for Jameson, whose bowling tends to be treated as a bit of a joke but who would clearly like to be considered as something of an all-rounder.

England's total was soon passed in the final session, as Rohan Kanhai began to inject the urgency the situation demanded. He thoroughly enjoyed his breezy little innings of 39, as, of course, did the spectators. But he showed that Englishmen aren't the only ones to get out to bad balls when he hit a full-toss from Greig straight to Willis at mid-on. By now the score was 401, and it was hardly a refreshing sight for tired fielders to see Gary Sobers ambling in to bat with that inimitable knees-bend walk.

But the great man was strangely quiescent, as too was Kallicharran, whose 89 not out was accumulated with uncharacteristic dourness.

The feeling that night was that England, though they had no chance of winning the match, now had a better than even one of saving it, but the events of the next day, the fourth, were to put the West Indies right back into the driving seat. It was Bernard Julien (whom some West Indians – though not ones from Trinidad – believed should not be in the side) who put them in command again. He had been promoted by Kanhai and came in during the first over of the day after Kallicharran had been caught by Denness in the gully off Old for 93. Julien announced his presence by hitting Bob Willis for three startling fours in an over, a fact which persuaded Denness into a premature introduction of spin, for the ball was still quite new. Julien tucked into Pocock and Underwood with still greater relish and he reached fifty in only 47 balls with a swing for six into the pavilion off Pocock.

Sobers at the other end watched his heir-apparent with lordly appreciation and was content to proceed himself in one's and two's. Julien's timing was extraordinary. Three times he leant forward, swung the bat casually through the line and lifted the ball effortlessly over the top of the bowler's head for four. But all good things must end, and Julien's innings did so when he chipped a ball from Greig to give Denness his second catch of the morning.

Sobers promptly reached his fifty. But after two legside fours Boyce flicked Willis to mid-wicket and when Sobers also holed out, off Greig for 57 – Willis holding a steepling catch – the fun was over for the morning. Willis had Barrett l.b.w. for a duck, and Kanhai declared at the lunchtime total of 583 for 9, a lead of 230.

England's reply was full of drama, with Boyce once again bringing this apparently somnolent pitch to vivid life. Bowling round the wicket on Kanhai's suggestion, he

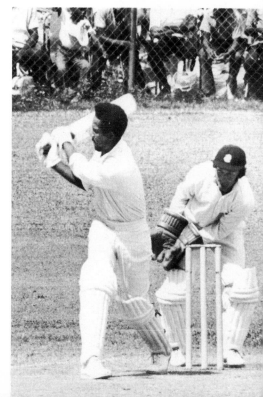

Variations on the sweep.
Above Kallicharran sweeps
Pocock at Bridgetown during
his record stand with
Lawrence Rowe. *Right* Sobers
prefers to stay on his feet as
he adds four more to his
record Test aggregate (first
Test, Port of Spain).

Left Dennis Amiss, hero of England's famous rearguard action at Sabina Park. This pulled four was one of forty in his superb 262 not out. Throughout he never missed a chance to score runs.

Below Characteristic postures in the early matches. *Top* Bob Willis displays his one-handed forward defensive stroke (first innings, first Test), while Sobers, Rowe, Murray and Julien watch intently. *Bottom* Underwood, who 'played like a suspicious bomb disposal officer': Sabina Park on the final day of the second Test. Amiss (of course) is the other batsman—Lloyd, Fredericks, Rowe, Murray, Kanhai and Sobers the close fieldsmen.

Frank Hayes hooks at Port of Spain (first Test). He was out
hooking or pulling more than once during a tour which was
bitterly disappointing both for him and for those who had
placed such high hopes in him.

unleashed a succession of menacing bouncers supported by a cluster of slips and three men deployed to gobble up any mis-hit hook. Amiss, in fact, hooked with success, smacking the ball off the meat of the bat with reassuring certainty. Just once was he troubled as he started out on what was to become one of the greatest of modern Test innings. He received one of Boyce's special bouncers which, unlike those from some bowlers which rise up in a parabola over the batsman's head, seem instead to slide through off the turf and to be directed like a guided missile exactly at the batsman's head. Amiss chose to raise his arms to avoid the ball and there was an appeal from behind the wicket, presumably on the grounds that the ball might have brushed a glove on its way. At any rate neither Amiss nor the umpire agreed and this sturdy man with forearms like tree-trunks stayed to offer an iron-grilled defence against the good balls and a clean cutting rapier to the bad ones.

This was to be one England fight in which Geoff Boycott did not play a leading role. Boyce produced a snorting ball which he tried to fend off but could only snick to the wicket-keeper. The next ball was as predictable as a comedian's catch-phrase: for the new batsman was Jameson. We knew Boyce would begin with a bouncer, and he did. We knew Jameson would hook, and he did. The ball flew off the top edge, and so short was the boundary at the northern end that it carried over slips' heads and into the crowd for six at third man. What would Boyce try now? Another bouncer, of course, and again Jameson hooked, this time more safely and for four. Burly, bubbly and belligerent, Jameson continued to flirt with danger, and when he had made 17 in the space of a couple of overs he was missed at second slip by Sobers off Boyce.

But Kanhai knows Jameson well and he soon had the spinners on. For a time the hectic activity calmed as

Jameson tried to puzzle out the flight of Gibbs and Amiss's bat began to flow with cover drives, square-cuts and those magnificent flicks off his toes to mid-wicket or square-leg. Occasionally he also drove straight, not with a full flourish but with superb timing, the power coming from the impetus of his high backlift.

Amiss reached his fifty with ten fours, a rousing start; but immediately afterwards his Warwickshire partner drove at Barrett's leg-break and the ball curled beckoningly to Rowe at slip.

Five runs later there occurred one of cricket's little tragedies. Amiss pushed into the offside towards, of all people, Clive Lloyd. He called for a dangerous, though not quite impossible, single. There was a tiny hesitation before Hayes, the quickest runner in the England side, answered the call. It was all Lloyd needed. From the commentary box it appeared that Hayes had just got home, but those who were watching from the pavilion thought that Lloyd's throw narrowly got there first. This, too, was umpire Cortez Jorden's opinion, given, on the run, after some hesitation. Poor Hayes: when a man's luck is out, it is really out. It seemed that another England slide had begun, and when the scoreboard bearing the names of the England batsmen came crashing to the ground in a strong afternoon breeze, it was somehow cruelly appropriate.

Fortunately Mike Denness now played extremely well whilst Amiss, not allowing the run-out to affect his concentration, continued to play with encouraging certainty. These two added 69 before, at 176, Denness, much to his surprise, was given out caught off bat and pad (a diving effort by Rowe after a call of 'catch it' from Murray). As the England captain walked out it seemed that all the hopes of a successful England tour were going with him. The impression of impending doom was strengthened when, fifteen minutes from the close, Greig was also out, bowled pushing forward to Gibbs, just as he had been at

Port of Spain. But as in that first Test, so here Amiss was refusing to surrender. When play ended he had made 123 not out; but England, still twelve runs behind, had only five men left.

Thursday February 21st was a good day for England: the day that Dennis Amiss, the quiet pipe-smoker who once looked so nervous in Test Matches that it seemed he would never be able to make the most of his abilities, and who even now had to take sleeping pills occasionally to stop his worrying at nights, became a national hero. It was also the day when English cricket rediscovered that the virtues of steely single-mindedness and stubborn pride can often be applied to resist more skilful opponents. Derek Underwood, Chris Old and Pat Pocock were also the heroes of a day's cricket in which England, against all the odds, saved not only the match but the series itself.

The day was hot and sunny. It rarely rains when underdogs are on the run. Kanhai tried eight overs of spin before taking the new ball, which was due at the start. In the very first over, off indeed the third ball of the day, Amiss turned Gibbs low and sharply to Sobers. The great man was very close at backward short-leg and the reflexes were not quite as quick as they had once been. Or perhaps it was just too early in the morning. At any rate the chance was missed and a match that might have been won by lunchtime was never won at all. Amiss never gave another chance. The ball hardly ever passed his bat for the next five and a half hours of play. He stood four-square like a yeoman soldier and, try as they might, the enemy could not get through.

Underwood, the night-watchman, played like a suspicious army bomb disposal officer, putting a tentative bat towards the ball and then withdrawing it swiftly as if he thought it would explode. Four byes from a swift legside bouncer from Boyce ensured that the West Indies would have to bat again and there was a spate of no-balls to keep the scorers active as Boyce strove for extra bounce and pace from a pitch which looked more docile than ever. This time he could find no hidden fire and Amiss and Underwood were still together after a first hour which had produced only 30 runs. Runs, however, at this stage were less important than a stubborn occupation of the crease. Underwood's innings of 12, for instance, looks ordinary on the scorecard, but he had batted in all for an hour and a half when he pushed out at Sobers and was taken behind the wicket by Murray.

It was reassuring now to see Alan Knott coming in. He had been short of runs, as everyone knew. But his spirit and skill had pulled England out of more than one hole since his brave rearguard action at Georgetown in 1968, the innings which had established his reputation. Today he had just settled in and collected six runs when Amiss pushed a full-toss short of Clive Lloyd at cover and, just as on the previous evening, ignored the fact that Lloyd is renowned as the finest cover fielder in the world. This time the supercat excelled even himself, picking up one-handed, pivoting and throwing down the middle stump, with Knott an inch or two short of his ground. (Poor Knott was to be run out again by Amiss in exactly the same way in the following game at Antigua.) These run-outs were sad blemishes on Amiss's innings, though his misjudgment was punished ruthlessly on each occasion by Lloyd; it should perhaps be recorded that Amiss also ran a lot of very good short singles – the margin between a good short run and a bad one being tiny. Incidentally, Lloyd pulled a muscle as he performed his master-stroke and nearly had to miss the third Test as a result.

Knott's tragic departure was, by the law of averages, the end. But the wicket remained easy, and Chris Old used a sound technique and a cool head to stay with Amiss, who was still looking for runs at every opportunity and thus always increasing the total that the West Indies would have to make. At lunch the lead was 64, England had three wickets left, and Amiss was 162 not out.

Afterwards the tense struggle continued, with Old doing much more than just surviving and Amiss looking sturdier than ever. But after making 19 and batting for 105 minutes Old was bowled by Barrett. Another two-and-three-quarter hours still remained. It was a tantalising situation, for another quick breakthrough would have left the West Indies time for a run chase. Pocock at first tested the hearts of the little band of English supporters who, with their incongruous straw hats, multi-coloured shirts and lobster-pink faces, stood out plainly amongst an increasingly frustrated crowd. But after Pocock had tried a few off-drives, in which the bat missed the ball by at least a foot, he soon told himself that this was not the time for spectacular strokes and he was still there when the indestructible Amiss passed 200 for the first time in his life.

The supporters of the West Indies had not totally given up even at tea, when England's lead was 145 with an hour plus twenty overs to go, but Kanhai and his team appeared three minutes late after the interval and it seemed they had resigned themselves to a draw. Umpire Sang Hue, a stickler for every rule, was so annoyed at having to wait in the middle inactive that he walked towards the pavilion in his dapper white uniform, looked ostentatiously at his watch and kicked the ball away in disgust. At last Amiss was given a few easy runs, but even fatigue would not get him out now and when the match was halted half an hour early he could relax at last. He had batted for nine and a half hours and hit 40 fours and one six. It had been a triumphant reward for iron-willed concentration and admirable batting technique.

Amiss had certainly saved the series because for England to have come back from being two-down (as they had under Hutton in 1954) would have been unthinkable. They had never looked like winning the match, and no one had expected them to do so. But they had done their morale infinite good by standing up at last to the immensely talented West Indian side. There were still plenty of problems. It seemed more unlikely than ever that England could bowl West Indies out twice and it was worrying that Old, Underwood and Pocock should have been able to bat for 105 minutes, 90 minutes and 80 minutes respectively when the specialist batsmen had again been all too hastily removed. But Amiss had bought time for his team: it was time now for the other batsmen to pull their weight.

Before leaving Jamaica I must make reference to one 'incident' in which I personally became unwittingly involved. The facts were misrepresented enough at the time for me to feel that I owe it to Geoffrey Boycott, to myself and, not least, to my employers, the BBC, to explain briefly what happened.

On the rest day of the second Test, I had been asked by my office to arrange an interview of topical interest. Up to this moment the Test itself had been a mild, generally unexciting affair, and the chief talking-point was the groin injury to Geoff Boycott which, following his arm injury in the previous game, was the latest in a succession of unfortunate blows to England's best batsman.

As is customary, I had a brief word with the manager, Donald Carr, as he was leaving the hotel with Boycott and the other players to visit a shirt factory. I asked for permission to have a chat with Boycott about his injury, and this was readily given. The injury in relation to the match was to be the main theme of the interview, but it was not stated, nor I think expected, that the conversation should be solely about his muscle to the exclusion of all else.

I agreed with Geoff to meet at lunchtime that day. In the event he was held up and was only able to talk on a tape-recorder some twenty minutes before the time of the circuit to London. I had it in mind to talk to him about the injury itself and about the wider problem of preserving himself from injury against short-pitched fast bowling. (I still have the bit of paper on which I jotted down four questions relating solely to those two subjects.) In the event Geoff said that he would prefer not to discuss his playing of short-pitched fast bowling lest it should reveal his tactics to the 'enemy'. We therefore discussed the circumstances of his latest injury and whether he would be able to field on the following day. In the hope of rounding off the interview neatly I then asked: 'Do you think that England should now save this game?'

Most players, I imagine, would have answered something like: 'Yes, there's no reason why we shouldn't. Who knows, we might even win' – a pleasant, but I suppose banal, end to an interview. Geoff Boycott however is not banal in any way and he answered at some length, arguing reasonably enough that as England were still some 200 runs ahead we ought to be thinking of winning the match, not saving it, and that more attention to getting wickets rather than saving runs would pay England better. He added that tactics on the field were not a matter for him but for the captain or vice-captain. In other words, he gave an honest appraisal of the situation and there was absolutely no malicious intention either in my questions or in his answers.

I checked that Geoff was happy with what he had said, as I always do. He said that he was, indeed actually added that no one could possibly take umbrage at his words – which in any case were an expression of what almost everyone was thinking at the time. I then had to hail a taxi quickly and rush to the studio, which I reached only just in time to play down the tape. Having done so I thought no more about it and certainly did not foresee that the interview would lead to trouble. This was originally to have been my first day 'off' on the tour, and perhaps I was getting a trifle careless: at any rate I fully accept that I *should* have realised that what Geoff had said *could*, if heard out of context, seem like implied personal criticism of his captain, and as such I should have played the tape to the manager. Unfortunately I did not sense any danger. My duty was to report the tour as fairly and as interestingly as I could, not to dig up 'sensational' stories.

Next morning, however, Boycott's words stirred a hornets' nest in London. Because of lack of time, always the number one problem for a broadcaster, my questions had been cut out of the interview, reference to Boycott's injury was omitted, and only the short final section of what he said had been used. The words in themselves would not have been inflammatory had they not been cued in with a reference to recent Press criticism of the tactics of Mike Denness, and also juxtaposed with another passage from the interview.

Newspapers did not arrive in the Caribbean until several days after they were printed in England, so I had not appreciated the extent of the criticism, nor had I foreseen this sort of interpretation of Boycott's words. The BBC reporter on duty that night, an international sportsman himself, certainly did not intend harm by using the material in the way that he did. As a journalist he probably did the right thing (though the juxtaposition of passages is only rarely justifiable).

It was an unfortunate chapter of accidents. Donald Carr decided to ban further interviews with anyone other than himself and the captain, and Boycott, myself and the BBC all received unwanted publicity. In fact, the Press criticism which followed was levelled mainly at the BBC and not at Boycott, but some of what was written was very much less than generous and stemmed apparently from longstanding grievances against the BBC. Those who claimed that the BBC has some special privilege in the game should remember the money which the Corporation gives annually to cricket and reflect that as broadcasting is a medium of the spoken, rather than the written, word, it is natural for radio producers to seek interviews with players.

Both I myself and the BBC sports office admitted that mistakes had been made, however unintentionally. But it is pleasant to be able to record that neither Geoff Boycott, who accepted the situation magnanimously, nor the authorities at Lord's allowed this one unfortunate incident to override the fact that BBC coverage as a whole has done much to foster the interests of cricket. In particular, they did not forget that the often-praised sports desks in the early morning 'Today' programme have attracted enthusiastic audiences for a long time and helped to give cricket, and cricketers, much good publicity.

6
Cricketing Houdinis: The Barbados Test

After the famous Sabina Park recovery it was natural that a match against the Leeward Islands in the holiday island of Antigua should be played in a festival spirit. Indeed such is the enthusiasm for cricket in Antigua that almost any big match is a reason for a festival.

The MCC party stayed in an extremely expensive but very good hotel, in a setting which is as romantic and beautiful as the most glamorous of travel brochures make out. The long white sandy beach, lapped by gentle blue water, has a background of swaying palm trees, and the hotel behind incorporates spacious rondeval-type rooms which look out onto lawns rather like a Cambridge College; a kidney-shaped swimming pool in the middle completes the set-up.

If MCC imagined that they would be able to enjoy this break from pressure by polishing off a weak Island side in a couple of days, they were soon disillusioned. There is no such thing as an easy match in the West Indies, and the Leeward Island team in fact contains some of the best young players in the West Indies. These include the subtle left-arm spinner with the lovely name, Elquemedo Tonitto Willett, and two men now learning fast in county cricket, Andy Roberts, the fast bowler who was soon to make his mark in Test cricket, and Vivian Richards, a hard-hitting batsman and useful off-spinner. These three all had good games as MCC struggled to gain a respectable score on the first of the three days, and then did their best to call the tune on an entertaining final day.

Jack Birkenshaw made a successful return to the side

after recovering from the cracked finger-bone which had kept him out of cricket for nearly a month. Birkenshaw, a friendly and humorous man, had remained cheerful throughout and it was good to see him playing a spirited knock in the MCC first innings and posing a few questions, as well as getting some rough answers, when he bowled.

Frank Hayes also made a welcome return to form. He struggled painfully on a damp wicket on the first day but on the second played some of those lovely strokes through the covers which had marked his entry into Test cricket in the previous summer. Keith Fletcher, too, made a few runs in the second innings but in the first he was bowled first ball by Roberts, whose rolling, menacing approach (though not his delivery) has about it a hint of Fred Trueman.

As for the MCC bowlers, none did better than Mike Hendrick, whose great virtue is that he keeps the ball right up to the batsman and gives it every chance to swing. Of course he was getting much less movement in the Caribbean than at home, but he plugged away manfully and looked as though he only needed an extra yard of pace to become an effective Test Match bowler. Tony Greig also bowled well again but it was as captain that he really shone. He was leading the MCC for the first time and he did so with relish and his customary enthusiasm and drive. Under him MCC certainly appeared to have authority, purposefulness, and awareness of what they were about.

One last word about Antigua before moving on to sterner matters in Barbados. For sheer bubbling involvement and enjoyment the spectators at the quaint and bumpy little recreation ground at St John's could hardly be matched. To see them dancing and cheering in the hot sunshine while Vivi Richards and Jim Allen were hammering Fletcher's leg-breaks and Birkenshaw's off-breaks to all corners of the island was to see the living definition of unbounded joy. Their uninhibited delight was impossible to resist; it was a moving expression of public pleasure, of the kind that the British reserve for a royal wedding or a coronation.

The island of Barbados, of course, knows all about cricket passion. The game is a part of its blood. Wherever you go in this tiny island, only twenty-one miles long by fourteen miles broad, you are likely to come across a game at any moment – near the sugar-cane fields, on the beaches, in the streets. Often the players are very young, sometimes there are as many girls as boys, and anything from a stick to a bottle suffices for a bat. These youngsters soon learn how to hit the ball, partly from instinct and partly from aping the famous players, whom they talk about as if they were members of the family.

Only a few youngsters ever play for Barbados, of course, and fewer still for the West Indies, though this is the island which produced Worrell, Weekes, Walcott, Sobers and many other great cricketers. But the remainder continue to play the game at weekends at lower grades, and when they grow too old to play they watch the game and talk about it. Like anyone or anything held in great affection, cricket excites them, indulges them, intrigues them, irritates them, makes them laugh and sometimes even makes them cry.

But there was nothing much for them to cry about during the MCC match. As if the great Amiss recovery had never been, MCC seemed to have gone backwards rather than forwards and they succumbed so feebly that Barbadan rejoicings after their ten-wicket victory (a repeat of a similar win against MCC in 1960) seemed empty.

Once again MCC were put in to bat after losing the toss, an indication not just of moisture in the pitch but also of a view generally held by now in the Caribbean that this was a shaky batting side which could easily be bowled out cheaply. Nor did MCC do much to correct the impression. Geoff Boycott, whose lowest score hitherto at Kensington Oval had been 90, was caught at second slip for two and only John Jameson played an innings of any spirit thereafter. Mike Denness made 56 and stayed with Jameson long enough to add 135 on a pitch which certainly justified Holford's decision by giving considerable assistance to the bowlers. Vanburn Holder used it well, as did the spinners – Holford himself and the off-spinner Albert Padmore who, from the start to the finish of his action, is an uncanny carbon copy of Lance Gibbs. But Denness was not at his best; nor was Hayes who, having reached fifty with the advantage, for once, of a lot of luck, became becalmed on that score for fifty painful minutes and then got out.

Jameson's innings in these circumstances was certainly a relief. He stood up and hit the ball well and with confidence, and it was only when he suddenly tried to resist the spinners with a series of ugly D'Oliveira-type shovel shots that he looked seriously vulnerable. Sure enough he was out trying to play this shot against Holford's leg-spin. After that MCC resistance was minimal, and if Barbados had not dropped several catches the total would have been less than the 270 it eventually reached.

Batting failure by this side was nothing new: bowling and fielding failures were less expected. Although the wicket had eased slightly by the second day Barbados, who lost their most experienced batsmen, Peter Lashley and Gordon Greenidge, for only 80 runs, should never have been allowed to reach a total in excess of 450. They had a very inexperienced batting side, and two young men who had been struggling to earn a regular place in it, Nolan Clarke and Collis King, were allowed to get away too easily. Once the initiative had been relinquished, Clarke went on to play the innings of his life, finishing the second day with a four and a six off the last two balls of the day to bring up his own 150. Earlier in the week he had scored his first century for Barbados in the match which clinched the Shell Shield Championship; he must have walked on air for a long time afterwards.

It would be pointless and unkind to dwell long on the inadequacies of MCC during the remainder of the match. Suffice to say that they lacked authoritative leadership in the field, missed their catches, failed to bowl to their field, and then in the second innings folded up feebly against splendidly hostile fast bowling from the bandy-legged Vanburn Holder. There was never a harder trier than Holder, but these same English players were used to playing him day in and day out in the County Championship without batting an eyelid. Suddenly his own determined efforts to get back into the Test side and MCC's readiness to surrender the initiative made him look like a world-beater. It was all very depressing – for the players, for their wives (most of whom had joined the party in Barbados), and not least for the plane-loads of English supporters who had swarmed in just before the nail-biting General Election in search not just of hot sunshine but of a rousing game of cricket. Instead they saw MCC sink to the nadir of their fortunes, and were left to hope that the Test Match at Kensington Oval would be a different story.

The Test began amidst a positive welter of speculation and fascinating experiment. The England selection committee – Donald Carr, Mike Denness, Tony Greig and Geoff Boycott – left out Frank Hayes and Derek Underwood. Keith Fletcher returned after missing the second Test through illness and John Jameson retained his place, which was only justice after his batting against Barbados. In place of Underwood, Geoff Arnold was recalled, the selectors preferring his experience to Hendrick's promise. Arnold seemed to have cheered up considerably since the arrival of his wife Jacky (so much for the diehards who believe that females have no place on cricket tours) and he was itching to justify himself.

The West Indian selectors, not completely satisfied that Keith Boyce's heel was cured, omitted him and included in their eleven not only Vanburn Holder, for whom a place simply *had* to be found, but also the 23-year-old Antiguan Andy Roberts, the first man from his island ever to be selected for the West Indies.

If this was a reason for excited conversation from the moment that the selectors made their announcement on the evening before the match, the events of the opening morning were even more remarkable. For much of the night there had been heavy tropical rain and to awake within a stone's throw of a palm-fringed beach and to see the rain pitter-pattering down, making little black spots on the surface of the gently undulating sea, was like participating in one of those Somerset Maugham short stories of the South Seas.

But once on the busy, bumpy road which leads to Bridgetown, lined on either side by trees and shrubs with exotic blossoms – hibiscus, bougainvillaea and the startling crimson poinsettia – one realised this was unmistakably Barbados: the more so as the little brown-painted houses of the thickly populated capital came into view. There are a quarter of a million people on this little island, yet even here it is possible to find relatively remote areas. The majority live in Bridgetown itself, and a good many of them seemed to be heading for the Kensington Oval on this first morning of the Test.

As at Port of Spain, so here, the air was damp and heavy and Rohan Kanhai, after winning the toss, put England in to bat. The decision was a psychological one, because the ball generally does not swing as much at Kensington Oval, a much more open ground, as it does at Queen's Park. But there was a small amount of moisture in the pitch and the first morning was likely to be the only time when either side, heavily packed with seam bowlers, would get much help.

England countered Kanhai's move with a piece of their own psychology. Geoff Boycott, who had begun the tour with a reputation as one of the world's best opening batsmen but who had looked so uncomfortable against the short-pitched fast bowling which had invariably been aimed at him, was dropped down to number four in the order and Mike Denness, with admirable phlegm and a determination to lead from the front, went in first himself.

Andy Roberts was given the new ball with Vanburn Holder and he bowled impressively. Frequently both Amiss and Denness had to hurry their strokes and more than once they were beaten. But they survived until a shower held up play for forty-five minutes. On the resumption Bernard Julien was called into the attack in place of Holder and he at once produced a superb ball which came back very sharply to take Amiss's off-stump. The hero of Sabina Park had made just 12 of the 28 scored at that point, and the excitement that followed his dismissal increased when Jameson inevitably hooked at his equally inevitable first-ball bouncer. The ball curved from his bat towards Holder at fine leg, but the difficult chance was spilled.

Roberts, who had also been unlucky when Denness had been missed off his bowling, was to have to wait another twenty-four hours for his first Test wicket, but neither Jameson nor Denness was able to capitalise on his escape. In the first over after lunch Jameson played a firm stroke from the middle of the bat off his legs. Roy Fredericks, with marvellous reflexes, got his hands to the ball and caught it behind him at the third or fourth attempt. It was the Guyanan's eighth catch of the series.

In came Boycott at number four, with Denness, struggling but still alive, as his partner. What a triumph if they could have shared a big stand! But it was not to be. Boycott looked reassuringly confident and solid, but when he had made ten Julien again got his wicket, finding Boycott's outside edge and giving Murray the chance to take a brilliant catch in front of first slip.

Julien had taken 3 for 22 in a devastating spell of ten overs and England sunk still further into the mire when Gary Sobers, bowling in similar left-arm medium-pace style at the other end, had Denness caught behind for 24: the end of a brave struggle.

At least one could say of this latest England collapse that good balls were getting the wickets. Fortunately Keith Fletcher now began to play the innings of authority which England so badly needed, and Tony Greig kept him determined, if not always comfortable company until tea. Afterwards Fletcher became yet another of Julien's victims. Again the ball left the bat, and again Murray took the catch.

But at 130 for 5 two Englishmen at last called halt to the latest West Indian victory march. Tony Greig was just starting out on a personal performance as colossal as the man himself. For sheer stamina and single-minded determination Greig's all-round performance in this match can rarely have been equalled. At times it seemed that only his iron will and intensely competitive spirit stood between the West Indies and humiliation for England. But today he found a man of equal determination and concentration in Alan Knott, who at last justified the continued faith which the tour selectors had placed in him.

Knott, indeed, was the first man to show clearly that this was a near perfect pitch for batsmen, true and easy-paced. When he is playing well he is a sweet timer of the ball, and it was a relief to see both Knott and Greig proceeding cautiously but comfortably. At the close of the first day they had added 89 together for the sixth wicket, and England, at 219 for 5, were breathing again.

The partnership soon became 100 on the second morning as these two applied themselves single-mindedly to their task. Knott played especially well. This was a man who bore no relation to the pathetic, prodding figure of earlier in the tour. In this innings his defence was safe, his attacking strokes sure and controlled. One square-cut off Holder left the bat like a shot from a rifle, and the Bajan crowd, who tend to be subdued when the opposition are batting, appreciated the quality of the stroke. But they are a crowd who love to criticise as well as to praise, and they expressed derisive disapproval when, at 257, Greig was missed at second slip by Sobers off Holder. It was a straightforward chance and suggested again that either the reflexes or the concentration of the great man were not as they had once been.

The escape seemed to quieten both batsmen, because progress was slow and cautious for a long time against steady seam bowling by Holder, Sobers and Julien. Knott himself sliced a drive close to Fredericks at gully, but a legside swing for four off Gibbs made this the record sixth-wicket partnership for England against the West Indies, and England lunched at 293 for 5, with the partnership worth 163. To the second ball afterwards Knott gave himself room to dab-cut against Lance Gibbs's off-spin and was bowled for 87. It was a highly risky shot, and the batsman paid the penalty.

Soon after Knott's departure, Greig reached his third Test century: a reward for sheer determined application and concentration. Old never looked like staying with him and was soon caught behind to present Roberts with a well-deserved first Test wicket. But Arnold, who is no rabbit with the bat, helped Greig add 38 for the eighth wicket. I had a word with John Edrich at the time – he was in Barbados with Jim Laker, leading a large party of English visitors – and seeing his Surrey colleague (not the greatest of hookers) having time enough to hook comfortably, he predicted a huge West Indies score.

His assessment was entirely correct but there was still plenty of English defiance to come before the West Indies began their next run spree. Greig continued to play responsibly, picking the right ball to hit with sound judgment. Twice he hit Gibbs for towering sixes, once over long off, once over long on. They were shots which illustrated the immense strength of Greig's arms, for he has a relatively short back-lift. But when his score had reached 148, equalling his Test highest, he played too early as he tried to turn a ball from Julien onto the leg side and was caught by Sobers. Even now England did not say die. Pocock and Willis played with plenty of spirit and good sense in adding 24 before the innings finally closed at 395, with Pocock caught on the boundary by Lloyd in the shadow of the pavilion.

England's total looked good on the board and after positions of 68 for 4 and 130 for 5 it represented a brave recovery. But the performance was almost immediately made to look fearfully banal as Lawrence Rowe and Roy Fredericks launched the West Indian innings with a series of superlative strokes. The 50 whistled up in eight overs as Rowe, starting out on one of the great innings of Test history, brought a hitherto subdued crowd to its feet time and time again. One quick-footed hook off Willis flew into the stand at square-leg with staggering speed – a thrilling, magnificent shot. But good bowling by Old and Greig put the brakes on his partner Fredericks, who was starting to look uncomfortable against Old when, much to the irritation of Mike Denness, the umpires called the players off twice in the last half hour for a sprinkle of rain and some bad light.

The rest day was followed by a weekend of memorable cricket and many records. Over all that happened two men stood out like colossi, and the contrast as they battled it out on their stage in the sun was fascinating to watch. For England, Tony Greig, following his face-saving century, bowled and fielded not just with his heart but with every fibre of his being. Never was there a harder trier. Against this warm-blooded, voluble, eye-catching enthusiast the West Indies pitted the cool, immaculate, inscrutable and masterly Lawrence Rowe. At last he laid the bogey which had haunted him outside his native Kingston as, not content with scoring his initial first-class century outside that ground, he went on to become the first West Indian to score 300 against England and only the tenth man from any country to do so in the long history of Test cricket.

Rowe had made 212 by the close of play on the Saturday as West Indies once again built an impregnable position. The day was burning hot, and the cricket was watched by the largest crowd ever seen at Kensington Oval. Nobody knows how many were there. The official capacity of the ground is 13,000, but there must have been present around 20,000, drawn to the ground by some instinct which told them that history was about to be made. By the start of play they were packed tight together inside the ground, overflowing into perilous positions on the roofs of the stands, with thousands more struggling to squeeze in past harassed gate officials. I was locked in a slowly moving scrum for fifteen minutes amongst many who were vainly waving their tickets: others pushed down a fence to force entry. It was remarkable that despite the intense discomfort in which most must have watched the cricket, there was no trouble beyond an occasional stoppage to clear bodies from inside the boundaries – and of course a periodical invasion of the field to congratulate Rowe on his latest landmark.

At the centre of this seething arena, the cricket was tense and balanced. Although England were able to take only three wickets in the day, they gave nothing away and Denness, in difficult circumstances, earned full marks for keeping his side at full pitch all day.

Rowe and Fredericks were unable to recapture the inspired mood in which they had started the innings with such momentum on the Thursday evening. Willis and Old began the attack, with Old delivering such a spate of no-balls that he had soon to be taken off. But Willis twice came close to yorking Rowe before Greig and Arnold came into the attack.

It was Greig, that jack-of-all-trades and master of several, who made the breakthrough. He moved the ball off the seam from the start and one which came back from the off glanced the inside edge of Fredericks's bat and hit leg stump. He had made only 32 of the opening partnership of 126 (there had been almost as many no-balls!) and for the second time running he and Rowe had put on over a hundred. For more than a decade West Indies had struggled to find an established opening pair but if Rowe had already solved this particular problem, he found a few of his own to solve on this second day as both Greig and Arnold posed awkward questions for him, especially around his off stump. True, his errors were few, but the excellence of the pitch helped to make it an uneven battle.

Some of the savage and elegant square-cuts and drives which whistled to the boundary at Kensington might have been turned into less savage edges to the wicket-keeper on England's green and not so pleasant pitches. But this *was* Kensington and on this day nothing could go wrong for Rowe. He reached his first century outside Sabina Park soon after lunch with a straight drive for four followed by a leg-glance for two, and the inevitable was acclaimed by tumult as hundreds of spectators sprinted onto the ground to mob and surround the triumphant batsman. Triumphant perhaps, but he did not celebrate with any undue excesses as he proceeded on the even tenor of his way down the hot afternoon. The ferocity of his attacking strokeplay contrasted with his calm, undemonstrative manner at the crease. So early did he pick up the line and length of the ball that it seemed impossible for him to become unbalanced or ungainly. On this pitch at least it mattered nought that he seemed almost exclusively a back-foot player.

At the other end Alvin Kallicharran lost little by

comparison. Again, the speed of eye and foot and the certainty of his attacking strokes demanded admiration. He hit seven handsome fours in his fifty as he and Rowe built a record partnership at a speed which at one stage became dangerous for England. But the bowlers stuck to their task well; Arnold especially had a long and marvellously steady bowl and the ground fielding was safe, even if at times the fielders were made to look painfully pedestrian by the superb timing of both players.

By tea the arrears were only 98, with Rowe past 150, and the arrival of Kallicharran's second hundred in three Tests was the excuse for another invasion of the field, though it was mildly resisted by a few good-natured policemen. When the second-wicket partnership reached 228 it became a record for the West Indies against England, and it was these two 25-year-olds who were again responsible for the massive total. After three Tests Kanhai, Sobers and Lloyd were all without a major score: they had not yet needed to produce one.

The record partnership was finally broken after tea – almost inevitably by Greig, who, having had one success as a seamer before lunch, now had one in his newly discovered role as an off-spinner. He bowled Kallicharran for 119, made in 271 minutes out of a stand of 249. Perhaps it was a pearl compared with Rowe's diamond, but it was a gem of an innings nonetheless.

Inspired by his success, Greig, in company with Pocock, made Rowe earn every run before the latter reached 200 with a hasty single to mid-wicket. He was clearly home as Jameson's accurate throw hit the wicket, but what the crowd's reaction would have been had he been run out one can only imagine. As it was, Rowe was again surrounded by ecstatic supporters, this time kept off the wicket by police. The best touch came when, after most of the crowd had been dispersed, a senior policeman, wreathed in smiles, personally shook Rowe by the hand and then ran off the field last of all, pleased as Punch at having exercised the privilege of the law.

It was strange, but indicative of England's staunch performance, that this day of West Indian triumph should have ended with the visitors on the attack, yet so it did. Clive Lloyd played only to survive. It is rarely the best approach, and it failed because the tireless Greig got a ball to turn and Lloyd edged a gentle catch to Fletcher in the gully.

At 394 for 3, the West Indies began the fourth day in a position which was already impregnable, and they ended it in one from which victory seemed almost a formality. Again, however, England did well for much of the day, keeping the West Indian scoring rate within reasonable bounds. Denness, who had wisely refrained from taking the new ball the previous evening (and who had done nothing to hasten a sluggish England over-rate, something which suggested a new hardness and pragmatism about his captaincy), had one more success with the old one on the Sunday morning. Of course it was Greig who got the wicket, and of course that wicket was not Rowe's but the much less prized one of Holder, the night-watchman, who was caught and bowled. Then, with the new ball, England had two more successes as Arnold, the deserving pack-horse, bowled Kanhai for 18 and Willis induced an edge from the bat of the great Sobers before he had scored.

What a catch it was too! The amazing Greig, like some circus performer who can play the clown, juggle, turn somersaults and walk a tight-rope all in the same act, dived full-length to his left (the difficult side) and clutched the ball in one hand an inch or two off the ground as it flew past him. What, one wondered, would this inspired and inspiring giraffe of a man do next? Walk upon water, perhaps.

But after the sublime exhibitionist, the simple per-fectionist again demanded attention. Rowe clipped two handsome fours in succession off Willis, and even when a ball from Old reared quite unexpectedly and hit him on the shoulder, his momentary look of effrontery was soon replaced by his normal untroubled calm, as he continued towards his 300 with the poise and balance of a master. After ten hours at the crease he became only the tenth man to score 300 in a Test, but just when we were beginning to wonder if the position of the match would allow him to tilt at Gary Sobers's world record 365, he was caught at deep mid-wicket by Arnold. This time the bowler simply *had* to be Greig, and he punched the air like a golfer who has just won the Open Championship with a putt of twenty feet and a last round of 66.

Rowe himself, the first West Indian to score a triple century against England, looked as cool and smart and fresh when he walked slowly out as he had when he had strolled in at the start of his historic innings three days before.

Julien, who might now have rubbed smarting salt into the English wounds, was out cheaply to Greig, but Murray and Roberts were allowed by Kanhai to bat until tea in a stand which added 40 runs. It took the lead past 200, but it also used up time which was valuable to the West Indies. Kanhai finally declared at tea at 596 for 8, and England thus went in 200 behind for the fourth successive Test Match.

The collapse which followed was predictable enough but, even to those hardened by English calamities, this particular one was startling in its suddenness. Denness again went in first instead of Boycott but in only the third over a ball from Vanburn Holder kept low and had him l.b.w. for nought. In the next Dennis Amiss played his favourite flick off his toes (a shot which, sooner or later, had to cause his downfall) and Julien, taking off to his left, held a catch almost as good as Greig's earlier in the day. The hero of Sabina Park was out for four and England were 8 for 2. Jameson and Boycott, beaten for pace more than once by Roberts, took the score to 29 before Jameson, who had looked relatively safe, was adjudged l.b.w. as he pushed forward to another ball which kept low.

Boycott and Fletcher now applied all their professional know-how in desperate defence but after a long scoreless period Boycott was caught off Sobers when the ball hit him full-toss on the boot, then glanced his bat and lobbed up to Kanhai at silly mid-off. It was an unlucky dismissal and at 40 for 4 the situation was almost hopeless. Boycott, whose lowest score at Kensington Oval before the MCC's return to Barbados had been 90, had now scored 2, 6, 10 and 13 there. The experiment of playing him at number four and Denness at number one had failed dismally.

As at Sabina Park, so here, England began the final day bound to apparently certain defeat by knots which would have severely taxed Houdini. Seventy-three for 4 was their score when Fletcher and Greig resumed before a sparse crowd. Perhaps the public had sensed another eleventh hour escape by England. Certainly, despite the long odds in favour of a West Indian win, there was not the same almost unbearable tension as there had been during Amiss's great innings in Jamaica, though England on this occasion did not save the game finally until some time after tea.

It was Andy Roberts who looked most likely to break through early on as he several times beat Greig for pace. But the shy, gnome-like figure of Fletcher was in polished and watchful control of almost all that came his way, and so he was to remain throughout the day. The first four of the morning did not come for fifty-three minutes, partly because of the extreme caution of the batsmen, partly because Kanhai had only one eye on taking wickets, the other on saving runs. Just occasionally the ball squatted dangerously, but after an hour in which 28 runs had been added Greig and Fletcher were still together. The chances for England were now increased by a heavy shower which held up play for forty-two minutes. Perhaps God *was* an Englishman after all. Certainly England were due for some luck. But only seven minutes after the resumption of play Greig, who had made 25, went onto the back foot to force Gibbs through a gap in his off-side field; as the ball turned he was unable to keep his weight over the ball and succeeded only in lofting it to cover where Roberts fell forward to take the catch. 130 for 5. It was not the first time that Gibbs had got a wicket in such a way in the series. He bowled with six men on the leg-side and so tempted the batsman to hit against the spin, often with fatal results. This artist of a bowler had lost none of his guile or his sinewy power of spin. There was an additional feature in the fall of Greig's wicket in that Kanhai had called up Lloyd to a close silly mid-off position. His looming presence there may well have encouraged Greig to play his attacking shot.

Kanhai suffered some criticism for failing to force a West Indian win on this final day, but it was hardly his fault. It would be both more kind and more accurate to give credit to the batsmen rather than to blame the captain and his bowlers. They did what they could, but Fletcher and Knott played outstandingly well. It was the assurance and positiveness of their play which made it less nail-biting to the partisan spectator than in the circumstances it should have been. Knott had one escape when he too tried to force Gibbs on the off-side and hit the ball hard at Lloyd's chest. Fielding very close at silly-point Lloyd could not get his hands to the ball. Knott was unaffected, and continued to look for runs with the perky industry of a sparrow pecking for crumbs. Fletcher, for all his Test Match disappointments, can at times look a player of the highest class, and he took the partnership past fifty with a square-cut quite as savage as any that Rowe had produced.

Both he and Knott continued to pepper the covers as the new ball came and went without another West Indian success. A no-ball at 200 brought the sides level and the partnership reached 100 soon afterwards. The personal landmarks followed: Knott's second fifty of the match in 114 minutes with seven fours, and Fletcher's third Test century in 298 minutes with 13 fours. Umpire Stanton Parris, a tall man with long Edwardian sideboards, who was standing in his first Test Match ahead of the experienced Barbadan umpire Cortez Jordan, had turned down a raucous appeal for caught behind off Sobers when Fletcher was 96. It seemed that Alan Knott might have caught the rebound, as it were, when he pushed forward at Clive Lloyd a little later and was given out l.b.w. Off the very next ball Lloyd clean bowled Chris Old and the crowd, hitherto almost totally subdued, began to leap and whistle and beat the rhythmic drums of victory. But it was really too late; Arnold avoided the hat-trick and played calmly whilst Fletcher batted safely through the first ten of the mandatory last twenty overs. For quality and richness of stroke his 129 not out had been almost as good to watch as his superb innings of 178 against New Zealand at Lord's in the previous summer. It was the positiveness of his play, and of Knott's too, which had been so satisfying. The match was saved not in a prodding, pushing way, but with skill and determination. As with those footballing sides who in the years after England's 1966 World Cup win came to Wembley only to draw, escape for England here was a kind of victory.

West Indies, without doubt the better side, had failed to win partly because of the excellence of the pitch, partly because of England's determination, and it was strange to reflect that had England only shown half the application in the first Test Match, the series would still have been level. As it was, the West Indian lead was only one, and now for the first time it was possible to imagine that if things were

to go right for them, and the old temperamental uncertainties of the West Indians were to return, England
might yet be able to salvage something more than honour
from the tour.

Not many Test Match draws are remembered for long. This
one will be. It contained Rowe's historic innings, and
signalled the arrival of a 'new star in the cricket firma-
ment'. It also included Tony Greig's great all-round
performance, as he became the first England cricketer to
score a century and take more than five wickets in an
innings. In addition there were a record number of
no-balls, two record partnerships – by Knott and Greig for
England and by Rowe and Kallicharran for the West
Indies – and two remarkable recoveries by England. All
these deeds were manna from heaven for the clinical
statisticians: but it was also the colourful setting and
highly charged atmosphere in which the records were
created which made the match so memorable.

7

The Tide Turns at Georgetown

Guyana, the former British Guiana, is as different from Barbados as Manchester is from Glastonbury, and the contrasts at once became apparent. The translucent blue of the Caribbean was exchanged for the muddy grey of the Demerara river, and the friendly, happy-go-lucky but commercially-minded Barbadans were replaced by the courteous, serious, politically conscious Guyanese.

Situated on the South American mainland, low-lying and close to the equator (as well as to Brazil and Venezuela), Guyana attracts few tourists. Here it is possible to contract tropical diseases like malaria, cholera, and yellow fever (though instances are rare); there are poisonous snakes, and it is dangerous to walk the streets at night, for 'mugging' and brutal robberies are common in Georgetown. One heard this so often, and from so many different sources elsewhere in the Caribbean, that it was a welcome surprise to discover a friendly if (not unnaturally) sensitive people, a hotel in which most things actually cost less than expected, and a city centre which is totally unlike any other. Laid out by the Dutch, tall, white-painted wooden houses with shuttered windows and red corrugated iron roofs stand elegantly by the side of splendid wide roads, and are bordered by tropical foliage of bewildering variety and colour.

The atmosphere in this part of Georgetown is still unmistakably colonial, even if today there are sharp tensions amongst the different ethnic groups; there is much talk of the third world; and modern commodities like bauxite, used in the production of aluminium, have assumed as much importance as old ones like sugar. As usual, cricket is a great force for unity, and no matter what the political differences were between Guyana and Britain the MCC party was greeted with the customary interest and enthusiasm. It is cricket which makes Guyana West Indian, rather than South American, and what cricketers this land has produced in the last few years! Kanhai, Gibbs, Lloyd, Fredericks, and Kallicharran all come from here, and in the Guyana match the touring side were to come face to face with some gifted new players, like Leonard Baichan, Romain Etwaroo and Fauod Bacchus.

What MCC needed most at this stage of the tour was a win; against Guyana they very nearly had one and in a two-day match in Berbice afterwards they at last achieved their first success. That they came close against Guyana owed much to a surprising declaration by Mike Denness which very nearly proved inspired. But in the end MCC were unable to open their account (after two months of trying) partly because of another easy-paced wicket, partly because of a remarkable performance by Roy Fredericks, and partly because of some ultra-defensive captaincy by Clive Lloyd. The latter did not look, on this admittedly scant evidence, to be the ideal man to take over the West Indies captaincy from Rohan Kanhai.

For the first time since the one-day match which had started the tour, MCC did not bat first and they must have appreciated the change as well as the excellence of the outfield at Georgetown's Bourda ground. There had been a lot of rain in the weeks before MCC's arrival and the grass was as lush and green as a field in England.

But in the pitch itself, and in the persons of umpires Kippins and Vyfhuis, lay the seeds of more frustration and trouble for the touring side. The pitch took slow turn from the start and so gave the two English spinners, Birkenshaw and Underwood, a chance to win back their places in the Test team. This they both did, but whereas Jack Birkenshaw visibly enjoyed the experience, poor old 'Deadly', for whom cricket at the best of times is an earnest struggle against inscrutable fate, almost literally burst with indignation as time and again he beat the bat, hit the pad, but failed to get an affirmative response from the umpires. In addition he was frequently called for no-balls.

One cannot fault the umpires for calling no-balls. It was soon established that their interpretation of the law was the same as that in England, and if bowlers are constantly overstepping the front line it is up to them to practise until they overcome the problem. But there can rarely have been a day when so many l.b.w. appeals were turned down. On flat, lifeless pitches the bowlers' lot is hard enough, and they can sometimes be forgiven for thinking that the stony-hearted attitude of the men in the white coats is sheer bloody-mindedness. All that can be said with certainty is that several of the decisions looked suspiciously close and it is easy to sympathise with one of the players who said after seeing Clive Lloyd being consistently beaten when trying to sweep: 'It's not fair; he gets a free hit every time.'

All this gave both Underwood and Geoff Arnold, who also felt harshly done by in the way of l.b.w.'s and no-balls, plenty of reason for irritation, and both men gave public expressions of their annoyance. Underwood snatched his sun-hat away on one occasion, and Arnold glared and muttered. This annoyed the crowd, who were delighted to find some new cricketers to bait and barrack, and revelled in their opportunity. It also piqued the umpires, who seemed all the more determined to put the bowlers in their places. The elderly Cecil Kippins, his crinkly grey hair covered in a white cork hat like those once worn by the British Army in India, countered Underwood's brief show of anger by ostentatiously chucking back his sun-hat after the following over and in the second innings he seemed so eager to no-ball Arnold that he peered round at the bowler as he came up to deliver. Arnold asked politely if he would not do this as it put him off. Kippins said he would not change his methods for anyone. Nor did he approve of Arnold's reaction because he then called over Denness to have a word with him.

To watch all this was highly amusing, but cricket is a matter of deadly earnest in Guyana and the local Press took the opportunity to lambast the British players for their 'unsportsmanlike' attitude. Most of the articles were reasonable; others, like the one which claimed that 'such monsters . . . should be grabbed by the scruff of the neck and hurled outside', were plainly absurd. The fact remains, however, that whether the umpires were right or wrong neither Arnold nor Underwood achieved anything by 'losing their cool'. Pompous moral principles aside, one of the first things one learns in cricket is that it is better to make the umpire one's friend rather than one's enemy.

The intensity with which cricket is followed in Guyana was given further illustration by a remarkable controversy which was raging furiously throughout the MCC visit. In order to raise money to pay for the erection of a new stand – a stand which it was hoped would raise the overall seating capacity of the ground by some 5000 – the Georgetown Cricket Club and Guyana Cricket Board had decided to sell life tickets at 350 Guyanese dollars (about £70) each. It was a policy which had worked successfully in some of the other West Indian countries, but in Guyana only a few were prepared to buy for life. Normally season tickets for the Guyana match and the Test Match were sold, but the Board had withheld them this year in the interests of selling the more lucrative life tickets. As a result it was faced with a defiant boycott and endless pleas over the radio and in the Press that its policy was an insult to the 'small man', who could not possibly afford to pay such a price. It was useless for the Board to plead that the

Anderson Roberts, the first Antiguan to play for the West
Indies, bowls a bouncer at John Jameson, who hooks his first
ball into and out of the hands of Vanburn Holder at long-leg.
Third Test.

Left Lawrence Rowe finally established himself in the eyes of the sceptical Caribbean public with his record-breaking 302 at Bridgetown. *Above* He off-drives Willis for four with typical grace and balance. *Centre* The end of a great innings as he hits Greig to Arnold at mid-wicket. *Below* Old is bowled first ball by Lloyd in the second innings of the Bridgetown Test. Fletcher, hero of another English rearguard, registers dismay.

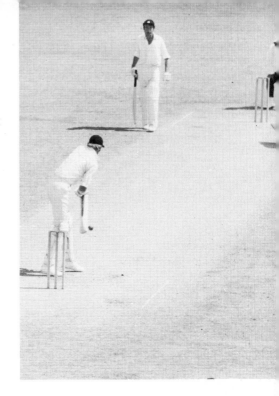

Right A contrast in styles as Greig (*above*) and Denness (*below*) struggle to combat the West Indian seam bowlers in the third Test. Denness went through a bad patch—he appeared to be playing with the bat too far from the body.

Above Tony Greig cover-drives during his century in the third Test. *Below* The old firm of Sobers and Kanhai dismiss Geoff Boycott, caught off boot and bat, as England collapse to 40 for 4 in the second innings at Bridgetown. The experiment of placing Boycott at number four in the order was not a success.

'small man' had never in the past bought season tickets anyway. They would pay at the turnstiles as they always had. But the Board still lost its case. After two of the stands had remained almost empty during the Guyana match, a weighty request from the Government persuaded the cricket authorities to release 280 season tickets for the Test Match alone at just over £5 each. People from all over Guyana began queuing at 4 a.m. for tickets due to be sold at mid-day and when the kiosks opened sales were completed within three-quarters of an hour. Many people, of course, were disappointed. They could only console themselves by remembering that, although there is no television in Guyana, both the radio stations carry nothing but cricket (except in the intervals) all day long during Test Matches.

This applied also to the Guyana match, one which attracted more interest from the locals, despite the boycott, than any of the other four-day games on the tour. It also turned out to be one of the best games, despite another slow and lifeless wicket. After winning the toss and starting moderately, Guyana were rescued and MCC frustrated by a fifth-wicket stand of 170 by Lloyd and Fredericks.

Fredericks went on to make a hundred – his fourth successive three-figure score for Guyana against touring sides – but like Lloyd and four other men in Guyana's first innings he was out to Jack Birkenshaw, who used the air really skilfully, something which Pat Pocock had been unable to do very often. Pocock had, especially after his good bowling at Trinidad, been rather a disappointment. A delightful extrovert as a man, he was perhaps not blessed with the shrewdest of cricket brains, and when the wickets had proved unhelpful to his classical, orthodox off-spin, his bowling had lacked strategy and improvisation. Against Guyana, Birkenshaw revealed a subtle flight which would not have disgraced Gibbs himself, and it was difficult to imagine Pocock having such extensive success in similar conditions, though on more helpful pitches he is perhaps the more dangerous bowler.

Guyana eventually made 393, Lloyd allowing the innings to meander rather aimlessly on with little acceleration, and the batting which followed from Amiss and Boycott was as good as any in the match. Boycott badly wanted a hundred and got one, but Amiss again outshone him, stroking the ball with wondrous timing. He made 108 of the partnership of 191, hitting 18 smacking boundaries, and when he was out it was a case of plodding prose following lilting poetry. (Boycott, when he had made 133, had to retire hurt with stomach pains.)

The game appeared to be quietly dying on its feet on the third afternoon when, to everyone's surprise, Denness declared 67 runs behind. Suddenly there was action, and moreover a chance of a result. Guyana were obliged out of honour to look for runs. This they did with rather exaggerated gusto, collapsing to 81 for 5 against no one in particular. For MCC it was heady wine. At last they had a side on the run and apparently in danger of defeat. But a determined and skilful little batsman named Fredericks denied them further progress. He went on to make his second hundred of the match, repeating his effort against the Australians in the previous year, and achieving the feat for the third time in his career. He thus proved himself again a much underrated player.

MCC did not bowl out their opponents in time to force a win, but there *was* time for Amiss to play another fine assertive innings and for Denness at last to do so too. Denness by this time had been virtually written off as a failure: a failure as a batsman, a failure as a captain. He had not communicated well – with his team or with the Press. People are harsh in such circumstances. They tend to forget the huge burden the man had been asked to carry. I preferred to think of him at this point as a disappointment, but a man who was learning fast from his mistakes. He showed in this match that there was still time for him to make the tour a success, not just for himself but for his team.

Before the fourth Test MCC went to Berbice for a two-day match against Guyana Second Eleven. They won the match, their first victory of the tour, but the cricket was almost incidental during the 48-hour sortie into the heart of Guyana's sugar country.

Two rivers — the Demerara and the Berbice — help divide Guyana into three counties. To the west, between the Venezuelan border and the Demerara river, is Essequibo county; in the centre lies Demerara county,and to the east, lodged between the Berbice river and Surinam, is Berbice county. At the mouths the rivers are so wide that ferries are the only means of crossing them and after travelling down Guyana's coastal plain for two hours the bus carrying MCC to Berbice suddenly bumped to a halt. Before them stretched the Berbice river, nearly two miles across and apart from the two landing stations at either side looking just as it must have done thousands of years ago. The jungle crowds to the banks with the outermost trees stooping over the water and with virtually no evidence of man's existence. There was an eerie peace about the river, and something strangely incongruous about an English cricket eleven coming to such a corner of the world. A poisoned-arrow team or a dug-out canoe crew would have been more in keeping with the 'African Queen' surroundings.

On the far bank New Amsterdam, the capital of Berbice county, came into view, about a mile back from the river. While the team was staying at a sugar plantation community centre, the Press party was booked into the Penguin International Hotel in New Amsterdam's main street and the players' mirth when the bus pulled up outside was undisguised. The building was indistinguishable from the other inelegant establishments bunched along the pavement, and inside it was some moments before the eyes adjusted from the glare of the sunlight to the darkness of a minute lobby. Upstairs the walls of the rooms were decorated with brown blodges where previous travellers had smacked to death pestering mosquitoes, and the sparse furnishing might have drawn a complaint from a monk. But the West Indian hospitality made up for the short-comings and even if one did not believe the waitress when the previous evening she took orders for 'a stream-lined breakfast', the enormous toothy smile was genuine.

When it came to bearing teeth the waitress had nothing on the alligators which moved stealthily about the stream bordering the ground where MCC's match took place. During the game two sixes were struck into this stream and the small boys who retrieved the ball checked first for the threatening stare of two bulging eyes. In fact, during the day alligators are seldom seen and it was after dark on the second evening that MCC went on their alligator hunt — an unscheduled expedition which might have produced an interesting reaction from Lord's had permission been sought. After all, when MCC were last in the Caribbean six years earlier Fred Titmus lost some toes in a motor boat propellor and back in St John's Wood they might have felt that an alligator hunt was pushing things too far!

The morning after the alligator expedition MCC resumed their match against the Guyanese second team, having the previous day declared seven runs behind on first innings. The declaration coincided with the end of a spectacular innings of 116 by Tony Greig, who scored the second 50 of his century in only 22 minutes with five sixes. Romain Etwaroo, the Guyanese captain, then set MCC a victory target of 237 in under three hours and this time it was a rollicking innings of 104 by John Jameson which thrilled the crowd. MCC coasted home by five wickets with nearly half an hour to spare. For Jameson and Bob Taylor it was the end of active cricket for the West Indies leg of the tour.

The fourth Test at Bourda began with a wholly new air of confidence about the England camp. They had saved two successive Test Matches, knew that their opponents were frustrated, and in Guyana had had the best of a drawn game and a win at last (albeit in a non-first-class match). Then, two days before the Test, they were given the marvellous psychological boost of an announcement that Gary Sobers had decided not to play. Sobers had told the selectors he was tired and that, though he would be available for selection again in Trinidad, he was not coming to Guyana. He had just played in a big golf tournament for Barbados, and those who knew him well thought that the real reason for his absence was that he was simply not interested in playing. Had the great man, like Bradman, ended *his* career with a duck?

In fact, he was to return for the final Test, but without Sobers the West Indies were inevitably a weaker side. He had not needed to score heavily with the bat, and had not done so. Even in the field he had shown a lack of concentration and had hinted that the feline reflexes were not as sharp as they had once been. But as a bowler he had been as dangerous as anyone and as both seamer and orthodox spinner he had had much to do with the win in Trinidad. Quite apart from what he had done, it was the fear of what he might do which really concerned England.

The reaction of the West Indian selectors was a wholly defensive one. Instead of reasoning that on a wicket at Bourda likely to be as flat and lifeless as the rest they would need an extra bowler to make up for the loss of Sobers, they instead chose Maurice Foster, a charming man and a very useful batsman but one of the world's most negative bowlers. (Approaching the wicket like a particularly flat-footed crab, he delivers quick-armed balls at or outside the off stump with a flat trajectory and invites the batsman to get himself out in desperation.) The promising Andy Roberts was omitted despite his auspicious first Test and so too was Holder, with Keith Boyce now fully fit and able to take his rightful place in the side.

England's batting line-up picked itself, for Jameson's disappointing performance at Bridgetown had made it almost inevitable that the almost equally disappointing Hayes would return – if only because of his much greater mobility in the field. The bowlers were not so easy to choose, and in fact there was a double change with Underwood and Birkenshaw replacing Willis and Pocock. In addition, Hendrick was named twelfth man. The selectors thought long and hard before replacing Pocock with Birkenshaw. They had made the mistake earlier in the tour of playing Pocock against Barbados when his finger was sore (against Pocock's own wishes) and, partly because he was worried by his finger, Pocock had not bowled so well in the third Test. Now, after Birkenshaw's success against Guyana, where he had taken 8 wickets in the match, the change was no surprise. Nor, in truth, was the dropping of Willis, sad though it was.

Willis had begun the tour as one of the main English hopes, suddenly, in the absence of Snow, England's fastest bowler and the main riposte to all the hostile speed with which the West Indies had so rattled England on her own pitches. But the pitches in the Caribbean gave Willis little chance to live up to expectations. Once he learned that he was not going to get any fire or bounce from the pitches, he should have sacrificed extra pace in the interests of greater accuracy. But with apparently little guidance from the senior players, and given very little bowling, Willis seemed to lose his stomach for the fight. Desperately keen to do well, he was unable to get into a rhythmical groove. He was troubled by bowling too many no-balls, and the usually poor net wickets did not help him to get over the problem. He would come again in Test cricket, but this tour which had begun for him with such high hopes had fallen about his ears.

If the tide was to turn in this match as the feeling in the air suggested it would, England needed to win the toss. This Denness did, though having done so his decision was not easy. To bat and build a massive first innings was England's soundest chance of winning. But the conditions were cloudy again, and there might have been some help in them for Arnold and Old. On each occasion so far the pitch had been at its most helpful to the bowlers on the opening morning. The consequences of such a gamble backfiring were, however, too awful to consider and Denness took the obvious course especially as there was no Sobers in the opposing attack. No sooner had he decided to bat than the rain started to fall. An hour and a quarter was lost before play could begin: an irritating delay for an excited capacity crowd.

When play began the pitch looked like a brown ice-rink and it literally shone – in sharp contrast to the lush, green outfield. The day began with a bouncer from Keith Boyce to Geoff Boycott, as had almost every opening day of every Test in the series. If the ball appeared to hasten through past Boycott's gently swaying head, the pace was deceptive. It was soon clear that this was another pitch of easy pace. Later in the over Boycott played a square-cut firmly for four, and England were on their way. In the next over Julien pitched short, and Amiss hooked him for four with the authority of a schoolmaster admonishing a naughty pupil. Already the boot was on the other foot,and so it was to stay.

England lunched after 45 minutes play at 26 for no wicket, and Kanhai soon introduced Lloyd, operating to a defensive field. But, out of the blue, Boycott aimed to hit

Julien through mid-wicket, played across the line of the ball and was bowled for 15. Julien could have been forgiven for thinking that Boycott had become his 'bunny'. Would he ever get a hundred in this series? Once again Amiss was to lead the way, and for the time being at least he had firmly assumed the title of England's number one batsman.

Denness, with greater confidence after his innings against Guyana, began more soundly than usual and played the faster bowlers with increased conviction. But occasionally he would make an inexplicable misjudgment. He must have smiled when Kanhai asked Foster to bowl ahead of Gibbs – for Foster would, in normal circumstances, hardly trouble the most ordinary of club players. When Gibbs did come on, however, Foster prevented four runs from a superb Amiss drive by diving full length to his left to save the ball and Lloyd and Julien were also outstanding as the West Indies gave nothing away in the field.

After the rainy start the weather had become oppressive – a hanging, enervating heat, and when Amiss took his drink with the rest at 76 for 1 he already looked a tired man with his shirt grey from sweat and clinging to his back. Meanwhile Denness announced that he had really found his touch with two handsome fours either side of the wicket in the same over from Gibbs. When Barrett came on for the first time in the 38th over, he was met with aggression from both batsmen, and they were still there at tea when England were 115 for 1.

Amiss reached his fifty from the first ball afterwards, a superb square drive taking him to his latest landmark after 161 minutes of concentrated effort at the crease. But at 128, with the partnership worth 87, Denness tried to late-cut Barrett; the ball came straight on rather than spinning away and fizzed off the bat onto the stumps.

Amiss had an immediate riposte, smacking Boyce

straight back past his shoulder for four. Julien was also reintroduced for the benefit of Fletcher, who had made only two when he edged just in front of Kanhai at slip. It took time for Fletcher to get going, as usual, but two beautiful offside strokes signalled his release from purgatory. Amiss by now was clearly tiring, yet his only sin was once again a liking for the risky single. He should have been run out going for his 94th run, but Kanhai's throw missed the wicket and flew away for four over-throws. Then, at 98, and with the new ball promptly being taken, Amiss was fortunate to be given the benefit by Umpire Vyfhuis as Julien rapped him on the pads and leapt in exhortation. But how Amiss deserved his sixth century of the tour, his fifth in first-class matches on the tour, his third in the series, and his sixth in all Tests! If Birmingham had decided there and then to erect a statue in his honour, he would have been worthy of it, and if the statue had stood as four-square as the one of Winston Churchill in Westminster, it would hardly have been inappropriate.

England ended the day at 218 for 2, and against a painfully slow over-rate and largely defensive fields it had been a heartening performance.

So England at last went into the start of a day, if not exactly in command, at least in a strong position. Their hope was that Fletcher and Amiss would take the score on to something like 300 so that England, with wickets in hand, might be able to accelerate in the afternoon and build up a position from which they would have a real chance of winning the match. It was not to be.

Fletcher is too good a player to start as badly as he so often does. He should tell himself to decide when playing defensively either that he is going to play a positive, solid defensive stroke – and a full stroke at that, not a prod – or that he is going to leave the ball completely alone. When he was out to a perfectly ordinary ball down the offside, it looked as though he was doing neither of these things, and he confirmed afterwards that he had been half-heartedly trying to do both. Sometimes he does not seem to appreciate his own abilities.

It was a little tragedy for England, and things got more serious when Amiss, after adding only twelve more runs received a bouncer from Boyce — the fourth that he had attempted in that particular over. Hooking at the ball too early he was caught behind as the ball touched his glove and curved in a gentle arc to Murray's gloves. Amiss had made 118 with fifteen fours, and the West Indies must have heaved a vast collective sigh of relief at his departure.

But this time they knew there was a longer, stauncher-looking England batting line-up to get through. Into the breach stepped Greig, with Hayes much more realistically placed at number six in the order. Hayes, however, had another bit of bad luck on his return to the side. While the rest of the team were celebrating their opening day success, Hayes was in bed with stomach trouble. It was thought when the second morning began that he might not go in as planned, but after the fall of two early wickets he did so and indeed started promisingly enough. When Lance Gibbs was introduced into the attack, Hayes moved down the wicket to his second ball and drove it sweetly to the cover boundary. But from great expectations sprang more disappointment. Hayes tried to force a short slow ball from Gibbs, played too early, and hit it straight back to the bowler, who fell and caught the ball beautifully in his left hand.

By lunchtime Tony Greig had already collected 29 runs and afterwards he began to hit the ball very hard indeed. A spanking straight six off Gibbs was the stroke of a man in form, a man in fact with centuries in the last two matches in which he had played, and on the way to getting a third one here. He got halfway to the boundary with another hard straight drive, this time off Foster who, like Lloyd, was being employed by Kanhai purely as a stock bowler to defensive fields.

Certainly these two bowlers were difficult to get away and even Alan Knott, who again looked full of confidence and who can be one of the great improvisers when it comes to scoring runs fast, was taxed to find ways to get the ball away. But his resort to the unorthodox was not unsuccessful. Several times he hit over the top of the infield, and once or twice swept Foster from well outside the off stump. At last, with these two going well, England were scoring at a run a minute as they had to do if they were to have any real hopes of winning the game.

Alan Knott reached his fifty with seven fours – his third successive Test fifty and an innings full of enterprise. But as if he sensed that his partner was taking too many risks, Greig suddenly went into his shell and sure enough two wickets fell quickly before tea. Knott tried to hit Gibbs over the top of mid-wicket but succeeded only in lofting the ball just over the head of Julien at mid-wicket. The latter ran back and judged the catch well. This brought in Birkenshaw close to the tea interval. He looked a little lost in the circumstances and after aiming two unsuccessful leg-side swings, he tried a third time and perished as he got a touch to a ball from Fredericks and spooned a catch to Murray off his pads. It was, remarkably enough, the first wicket that Fredericks had got in a Test Match. It was a surprise that this skilful purveyor of chinamen and googlies had not had more success.

Now West Indies were amongst the tail, but Tony Greig managed to keep firm control of the way things went. He found his touch again after tea and played some superb strokes through the covers. Chris Old began merrily enough against the spinners, whom he plays well, and despatched one short ball from Fredericks into a nearby road with a clinical swing over square-leg. But he plays the fast bowlers very much less comfortably and once the new ball was taken his days were numbered. He was unable to add to his score for four overs, then snicked Boyce hard and straight to Kanhai, who made no mistake at first slip.

Greig went on to reach his fourth Test hundred and his second in successive Tests with two fours through the covers off Julien. It had been an innings of mixed moods but very few false shots, and he had hit the ball extremely hard when making up his mind to attack. Arnold kept him solid company for a time before running himself out for one and only in this last half an hour was it possible to doubt the England tactics. Denness chose to bat on and get as many runs as he could when some would have preferred him to call for an acceleration and then try to give the West Indies an awkward half an hour's batting. As it was Greig finally perished for 121 with only seven minutes of the day's play left and the West Indian reply was postponed until Sunday.

When they did bat, it was soon confirmed that the whole atmosphere of the series had changed. Against tight, hostile bowling the West Indies batsmen were struggling from the start and England were unlucky when -- at ten to three -- a heavy fall of rain ended play for the day. Arnold and Old began the bowling to Rowe and Fredericks and this time there was no runaway start. The morning was overcast and threatening, the ground jam-packed, as it had been since six in the morning. Each time that Rowe or Fredericks moved into an attacking shot, the crowd gave a great belly-roar but time and again their strokes were directed straight to a thoughtfully placed field. Only thirty came in the first anxious hour. There had been some good shots, but some close l.b.w. shouts too, and when he had made 15 Fredericks seemed for a second to have been caught by Greig off Underwood. The ball had come off the boot, but in the next over Rowe cut at Arnold and Knott, diving to his right in front of slip, could not quite hold on to a low chance.

Fredericks was very much the senior partner today as Rowe, watched by his father, a gaunt-faced proud old man whose expenses were being paid by the Jamaican Government, played a studious defensive role. Then Fredericks himself was missed, again by Knott, a nasty low snick as he pushed out at Underwood. Just as it seemed that England would go to lunch without the success they deserved, Rowe tried to chop the penultimate ball from Greig, bowling in his off-spinner's style, and played it onto his stumps. This time Greig's punch of triumph to the crowd seemed superfluous.

Now the crowd settled in to watch the two local left-handers, Fredericks and Kallicharran. So far Kalli's first innings knocks had produced two fine centuries and a subdued ninety, and when he stepped back to whip a slightly short ball from Birkenshaw through the covers for four he seemed to be on his way again. But Birkenshaw had earned his wicket in the Guyana match by his skilful flight, and now he did so again. Giving the ball a tempting extra inch or two of air, he lured Kallicharran out to drive. The bat flailed at empty air and the ball passed through to hit the wicket as Birkenshaw leapt in sweet triumph.

When he came off to give Old a chance to blast through the defences of Kanhai, the new batsman, Birkenshaw had taken 1 for 14 in eight overs and had already done much to justify his selection. Kanhai had come in ahead of Lloyd, perhaps to try to unsettle the bowlers with a left-hand, right-hand combination and the crowd knew that this was probably to be his final Test on his home ground. The captain saw the 100 up in the 46th over, but the tension returned when Old, athletic and menacing, came back into the attack. Once, Kanhai left a ball which shaved his off stump, and then Fredericks looked desperately close to persuading even Sang Hue that he was l.b.w. Soon afterwards, at 110 for 2, with Fredericks 58

not out and Kanhai 11 not out, the rain which had long
been threatening came down with such remorseless force
that the crowd which had waited so long in the early
morning soon knew their. entertainment had ended prematurely.

The England team had plenty of time in the next two
days to wonder what might have been. The rain continued
long into Sunday night, and when we awoke on Monday,
the rest day in the match, the skies were again low, grey
and heavy with moisture. For much of the day it rained
again, and then on the fourth day there was the depressing
business of hanging around in warm sunshine while a listless
groundstaff fought a losing battle with an outfield which
in places, especially around the practice net pitches, was
like a paddy field. The pitch itself, despite the slender look
of the tarpaulin covers which had been its only protection,
was dry as a bone and, looking at it, one wondered
whether West Indies could possibly have lost the match
even had they been forced to bat on it for two days.

Many of the England team did not even bother to
depress themselves further by travelling to Bourda to
watch the tedious and futile operations. Mike Denness,
duty-bound to be there, was friendly and relaxed, taking
his disappointment staunchly, a happier, more confident
man than the anxious detached figure who had seen his
team stumble from crisis to crisis earlier in the tour, like a
seaman on his maiden voyage as skipper with a rudderless
ship to steer. Now foul weather was threatening to push
the ship off course again, just when the master was
regaining control and the crew were pulling together.

The final day was again sunny, but once more the
morning was spent in tedious limbo. (Not the West Indian
kind of limbo!) There is nothing more depressing than a
cricket ground on a sunny day with no cricket being
played. Little groups of spectators sat chatting together in
subdued tones, the normal fire and animation of their

Caribbean cricket talk drawn by the boredom of their long wait for the action to begin. The groundstaff sat in the middle of the pitch, waiting too, with the canvas covers rolled up beside them. They had done all that was possible, laying down sawdust on the damp areas of the outfield and rolling them out until they were flat and almost dry.

Now it was up to the umpires, Sang Hue, small and expressionless, and his partner, Compton Vyfhuis, a thin, anxious-looking man who had looked as sound and authoritative as any of the second strings chosen to stand with Sang Hue in this series. The captains had played the ball into their court, and the decision was theirs alone – a decision anxiously awaited by the West Indies Cricket Board who must have lost a good deal of money because of the rain.

Eventually they were able to begin play at 1.50, but by now the Wisden Trophy was safe in West Indian hands for another few years. On the evidence of the greater part of the series it undoubtedly deserved to remain there. The final Test in Trinidad would determine the honours of the series.

There was little point left in this particular match beyond providing some entertainment for cricket-starved and remarkably patient spectators. For the England team there was now nothing to gain, indeed a fair bit to lose, in terms of initiative, and despite a very considerable crowd of several thousands there was an unreal air about affairs as play began again after eleven and a half hours of playing time had been lost since the delay on Sunday and over twelve hours – two full days – in all since the start of the match.

If England had nothing to gain any more, West Indies now had the chance of some valuable batting practice. Roy Fredericks, 58 not out, had already scored successive hundreds in the Guyana/MCC match and had little to prove, but Rohan Kanhai was badly in need of some runs

113

to boost his confidence. At this late stage of the West Indian season he had yet to score a single fifty and there was a general belief that his 78th Test Match would indeed be his last on his home ground at Bourda.

He played some good shots, but the pitch was doing enough to make the England spinners wish even more strongly that they had not lost so much time. Roy Fredericks played them well and when he got to 98 it seemed that he was sure to reach his third Test century, but Tony Greig is not a charitable man on a cricket field at the best of times and certainly not in a Test Match. He induced a check drive from Fredericks, and then dived forward to hold the return catch inches from the ground in his left hand. So close to the ground did he hold it that Fredericks did not walk, but the uplifted finger of Umpire Vyfhuis sent him reluctantly on his way. The more so no doubt, because Fredericks had large financial incentives to score a hundred. Never mind, he did win something for being named the man of the match on the West Indies side.

For the second Test in succession there was no doubt about England's man of the match. Tony Greig had made a hundred almost as authoritative as his memorable century against New Zealand at Trent Bridge in 1973 (oddly enough, Dennis Amiss was the other English centurion in that game too) and now he was again bowling his off-cutters with skill and effect. His ability to bowl, like Sobers, in two styles had given England a valuable extra card to play with.

It was Derek Underwood, however, who had the final success of the match. The players, as was only right, had continued playing through a short shower, and perhaps it was the effect of the sun which followed, working on the dampness, which made the pitch suddenly do enough to worry Kanhai and Lloyd. These two had offered the crowd no fireworks and in the final over of the match Underwood got a ball to bite and turn past Kanhai's forward defensive stroke. Wickets had been hard to get for Underwood on this tour, and his leap of joy as he saw a ball doing what he wanted — and for good measure hitting the stumps — was easy to understand. He later described this as one of the best balls he has ever bowled. It was only right, too, that the match should finish with an English success, though the warm evening sunshine made the rain which had gone before seem all the more galling.

So to Trinidad for the final showdown.

8
The Decider: The Second Trinidad Test

The MCC party lost no time in getting to Trinidad. The days of rain-induced inactivity had been a frustrating waste of time, and the team flew out from Georgetown on the short journey to Port of Spain early on the Thursday morning of March 28th to make sure of a good practice session at Queen's Park Oval. In fact Geoff Boycott, ever keen to get in as much practice as possible, had organised an even earlier flight for himself, on the Wednesday evening. Through a telephonic misunderstanding a seat was booked for him in a plane bound for Chad in Central Africa. Fortunately the error was discovered in time, but the imaginary picture of Boycott arriving, bat in hand, at an airport in darkest Africa is a priceless one.

The only fitness doubt once again surrounded Chris Old, who seemed to strain a muscle in some part of his body in almost every match he played. There was an anxious wait on the eve of the match before, following a morning in the nets and a final selection meeting, England announced their side. Old was ruled unfit and Willis and Pocock were added to the remaining ten that had played in Georgetown. The decision whether to go into the match with an overloaded spin attack and to omit Willis, or to take the gamble of including him at the expense of one of the spinners was left until the last possible moment.

The West Indies had named a squad of fifteen players. Gary Sobers was welcomed back for what seemed sure to be his last Test appearance, and Vanburn Holder and the two Trinidadian spinners Inshan Ali and Raphick Jumadeen were also included. Local rumour had it that it would be the orthodox spinner Jumadeen who would play, but for once the grapevine had got things wrong, because it was Ali who was named in place of Barrett. Inter-island cricket politics certainly had a part to play in the selection of Inshan, but after a disappointing showing in the first Test he had bowled Trinidad to success in devastating manner in the win over Jamaica – a result which enabled Barbados to win the Shell Shield outright. So the West Indian eleven was the same as the one which had been successful in the first Test. There was no doubt a certain superstitious comfort for the home side in this fact alone, but the words of Clyde Walcott on the eve of the third Test came back to me then: 'I would not like to go into the last Test Match only one-nil up in the series . . . Anything can happen in Trinidad.'

It *was* anybody's match, and we all knew it. Of only four matches to have had a positive result in the four most recent seasons of Test cricket in the Caribbean, three had been at Port of Spain. But, even over six days – the extra day having been agreed at the outset of the tour in the event of the series still being undecided – a definite result here was no foregone conclusion. Both India and New Zealand had drawn with West Indies in six-day Tests in Trinidad in recent seasons. There was a chance of rain again, and whereas England had to win or bust the West Indies would be content with a draw. Nevertheless there was a general feeling that for them to approach the match defensively would be playing into England's hands. With so much at stake and so much less between the two teams now than there had been when England had stumbled out of form and disorganised to defeat two months before, a great Test Match was indeed about to unfold.

Saturday dawned bright and sunny. In England the match was competing against the Grand National and the FA Cup semi-finals. But in Trinidad only one thing mattered. When my breakfast arrived later than usual I was told that the hotel was short-staffed as one of the waiters had been shot the previous night – in an argument about the Test Match.

Surprisingly there were a few empty seats as Kanhai and Denness went out to the hard brown strip to toss. The subdued applause soon told us that Denness had called right, and having done so he did not have to think before committing England to take first strike for the fifth successive time. England had decided to leave out Willis and thus played an attack heavily overloaded with spin. The decision might have been regretted had Kanhai won the toss and batted, but if there were a little moisture in the pitch it did not concern Amiss and Boycott as they cautiously negotiated the opening overs from Boyce and Julien. Boycott, still looking for his first hundred in the series, took most of the early overs, studiously avoiding anything pitched short, offering a solid defensive wall against everything else. With six days to go there was no hurry, although Amiss twice swatted at bouncers from Boyce without connecting. Generally the start was slow but sure, and the most serious alarm of the morning came when Boycott and Amiss got themselves into a state of total confusion over the running of a leg-bye. First Amiss was almost run out at the striker's end, then Boycott was even closer to being dismissed at the other. Somehow he won his sprint to the crease against the ball and for his pains suffered only a slight bruise to his arm and a rather greater bruise to his dignity.

Later in the morning Deryck Murray was more seriously injured when struck above the eye by a ball down the leg-side from Inshan Ali. Play was held up for six minutes, Murray was taken off bleeding, and Rohan Kanhai, a former Test wicket-keeper, accepted the role again with some relish. Inshan, introduced into the attack when England, after 70 minutes batting, had made only 24, began with three testing maidens. But when he pitched short Boycott and Amiss despatched him for effortless fours in the same over and the nature of the pitch seemed to be clearly categorised already as yet another easy-paced turner.

Two beautiful offside fours by Boycott, a drive almost straight and a force through the covers off the back foot, took England to lunch at 64 without loss, Boycott 32 not out, Amiss 28 not out. The first foundations of a tall score had been carefully laid.

After lunch, however, Boyce was unleashed again, testing Boycott with short-pitched balls bowled to a curiously defensive field. One uncertain fend-off by Boycott seemed to force him into still greater caution, because for fifty minutes after lunch he was unable, indeed seemed hardly willing, to add to his score. It was as if he were digging himself in for all six days of the match. Amiss showed greater urgency and it was this which got him out. Sobers was bowling wide of the off stump to a strong offside field and when he had made 44 Amiss cut at a short one and edged into Rohan Kanhai's waiting gloves. No specialist 'keeper could have done it better. England were 83 for 1 and this was Sobers's 100th wicket against England.

Some smart fielding, especially by Julien and the emergency fielder Foster, kept the pressure on when Denness came in, but Kanhai was restricted in his permutations by the fact that Keith Boyce had had to go off the field with a strained calf muscle. Murray, however, was able to take up the gloves again an hour after lunch and to turn his attentions to the tricky spin of Inshan Ali.

In the period until tea Inshan went some way towards justifying his selection. He bowled seven overs, conceded only four runs and took the wicket of Denness. The England captain, for whom this was a vital innings in a decisive Test Match, had started on his way with a firm leg-side crack off Gibbs, but he was not the only player to look a little uncertain at times about which way Inshan would spin the ball next. When he had made 13 he pushed forward and edged into the sure hands of Roy Fredericks at forward short-leg.

Boycott, subdued but composed, was still there at tea, 57 not out after four hours at the crease. Perhaps England had been too cautious for their own good, yet it was a lack of caution which accounted for Keith Fletcher. He hit a fine on-drive which looked like a four until Clive Lloyd swooped on the ball and prevented even a single. Perhaps frustrated, Fletcher danced down the wicket to Gibbs's next ball, went through with a dangerous attempt to hit over the top of the onside field, and lobbed a catch to Kanhai at mid-wicket.

The manner of Fletcher's downfall did not discourage Tony Greig from an equally aggressive approach. He began with a firm drive over mid-off and generally seemed to be relaxing the pressure on his side when he swung across a straight floater from Gibbs, was struck on the pads full-toss and given out without a second's hesitation by Umpire Ishmael. At 164 for 4 England were struggling.

Frank Hayes came in at this awkward moment, with 45 minutes of the day to go, the new ball due and a question-mark hanging over his head as a Test cricketer. The new ball, in fact, had been available to Kanhai for some time and he took it finally after 95 overs. Though Lance Gibbs had only been able to turn the ball extremely slowly (Boycott frequently having the time to step back and hit him against the spin into the offside field) he had still returned figures of 2 for 52 from 27 overs and his ageless skills and constant changes of pace had adorned a dull afternoon. Inshan Ali had once again proved expensive in the long run, his one wicket costing him 72 runs from 29 overs. As for Sobers, he had been treated with exaggerated respect by Boycott, and now he was to take the new ball and to make it talk.

There was a school of thought which believed that Sobers should always have been given the new ball in this series, but the success of Bernard Julien had justified the preference usually accorded to the younger man. Now with Boyce unable to bowl at full blast Sobers showed what a superb artist he is. The first new ball had moved hardly at all. But with this one Sobers was at once causing Boycott difficulties with late inswing and the occasional ball flying away across the batsman towards the slips. Boycott by this time was so firmly entrenched that it would have taken an inspired ball to dismiss him, but at the other end Hayes was close to being l.b.w. when he padded up to Julien's inswinger. There was a further delay in play when the unfortunate Hayes was stung by a wasp, but in the end he was able to draw the sting of the new ball and the only remaining question on this opening day of the match was whether or not Boycott would reach his hundred. With almost masochistic relish he denied himself that pleasure and strode out, head up, 97 not out at the end of a day on which England had been able to score only 198 for 4 in six hours. They had not won any new friends, but time would tell the true worth of their efforts. On this day, of course, England's performance was one and the same thing as Boycott's. Had we seen the first instalment of a match-winning innings? Or had his batting been just too cautious and painstaking for the good of his team? Much depended on how his innings, and England's, developed on the second day.

As it turned out, Boycott could add only two more runs, and England collapsed sadly. Frank Hayes was unable to resume his innings because of a recurrence of the tummy upset and vomiting which had afflicted him in Georgetown. So it was Alan Knott who accompanied Boycott to the wicket. Boycott was clearly tense as he strove to get three remaining runs needed to give him his thirteeth Test hundred but his first for some time. It was not to come. After twenty minutes he played the thinnest of leg-glances to a ball from Julien and Deryck Murray took off the ground to his left to catch the ball one-handed at full stretch. In a series full of brilliant catches this was one of the best and certainly one of the most significant. Murray is an underrated cricketer. As a batsman he is a consistent run scorer who plays sensibly within his limitations, and as a wicket-keeper, though he can sometimes look untidy, he virtually never misses a chance. He certainly made fewer errors in this series than Alan Knott.

On Knott the batsman much now depended. He soon lost Jack Birkenshaw, who played one authentic four through the covers, snicked another through the slips, and was then caught off the shoulder of the bat from a sharply rising ball by Julien. It was Julien's thirteenth wicket of the series, and with Gary Sobers playing his swan-song West Indians must have been comforted to know that his obvious successor was now a fully mature Test cricketer.

Hayes now came in again and added twelve to his overnight score in a much more assertive manner. But when he tried to cut Inshan Ali he succeeded only in directing the ball straight to Rowe at slip. This was a straightforward catch, but the West Indian fielding all through the innings had been of a very high standard and two pieces of Clive Lloyd's own special genius were now to bring an abrupt end to the England innings. Geoff Arnold looked quite capable of staying with Knott and had made six without any discomfort against the spinners when he was superbly run out. Knott played a ball from Ali into the covers and set off a yard or two down the wicket. Arnold, backing up, also came up the pitch a few yards. A moment's hesitation before he turned to regain his ground was enough for Lloyd, who swooped on the ball and, for the third time in the series, threw down the wicket.

A few minutes later the supercat was at his tricks again,

leaping across the pitch from close silly mid-off to hold a spectacular bat-and-pad catch off Inshan Ali. Pocock looked as startled as a captured mouse. When, on the stroke of lunch, Underwood was bowled for four by Gibbs, England had lost their last six wickets in the morning session for 69 runs. Dreams of a total around 400 had dissipated into the reality of a moderate score of 267. Alan Knott, who had played very well but had not attempted to protect the tail when it patently needed careful tending, was left 33 not out.

Fredericks was soon giving a confident air to the all-important West Indian reply, but while he began with some firm drives off Arnold, Tony Greig soon had Lawrence Rowe in considerable difficulties at the other end. With marvellous versatility Greig switched back to his seamer style as if he had been opening the bowling for England all tour. More than once Rowe mishit his favourite cut stroke close to the stumps, and on another occasion he edged the ball first-bounce to Knott behind the wicket. But England were out of luck. West Indies made 36 in the first hour and the nearest thing to a chance as Rowe and Fredericks built their third century partnership in four attempts came when Fredericks, then 36, mis-hooked a delivery from Arnold. The ball flew off the edge close to Knott, who seemed to mistime his dive and was unable to get a hand to the ball. Fredericks proceeded to his fourth fifty of the series with a sweep off Birkenshaw, and after tea the hundred came up without a success for England. The spinners, however, who were queuing up to bowl, were beating the bat enough to give real hope and at 110 Pocock broke through. First he induced an outside edge from Fredericks and Fletcher held a good high catch to his left at slip. Then, at 122, came the greater prize of Kallicharran. After his recent low scores Kalli began cautiously; his first attempt to score brought about his downfall. He drove Pocock hard, low and straight and the bowler took a fine return catch.

Now came one of the crucial periods of the match. If England could have pressed home their sudden advantage with two more wickets before the close the game would have been very open. The new batsman, Clive Lloyd, was clearly keyed up, prancing about the crease like a caged tiger, and he was almost caught and bowled from his first uncertain scoring stroke off Pocock. He was lucky again when he swept high towards Boycott at deep square-leg, but Boycott seemed unable to pick the ball up in the low evening sun and it fell harmlessly in front of him. Then, when he had made twelve, Lloyd survived a confident appeal from the England close field for a bat-and-pad catch. In both cases Underwood was the unfortunate bowler, and although Rowe played better and better to end the day 75 not out the England spinners had done enough to encourage the belief that the match was not yet completely cut and dried.

The West Indies resumed after the rest day 93 runs behind England with eight good wickets in hand. It was a strong position, though not yet a cast-iron one. The new ball was due after ten overs and on an overcast morning Denness had a ticklish problem of when to take it. He opened with Pocock and Underwood and on a pitch now bone dry there was plenty to encourage them. Clive Lloyd, without a fifty to his name in the series, again looked nervous and uncertain and Rowe's first boundary was a risky sweep which passed just over Greig's head at backward square-leg.

A sharp shower after half an hour held up play for fifteen minutes and seemed to do wonders for Clive Lloyd. He suddenly produced an array of shots against Pocock, though Underwood, now bowling at his very best again, gave nothing away at the other end. Jack Birkenshaw, the other 'form' bowler, was not called upon – underlining the problem a captain has when his attack is overloaded with bowlers of the same type. In the event Birkenshaw was not to get a ball all day, for Tony Greig was about to begin one of the most famous bowling spells in Test history.

His brief bowl before lunch gave little indication of what was to come. A second and more prolonged shower allowed only 46 minutes play in the morning session and by now, at 208 for 2, the West Indies were approaching an invincible position. Still resisting any temptation to take the new ball Denness began after the interval with Greig from the pavilion end and Underwood from the other. Underwood continued to bowl beautifully, conceding only three runs from his first seven overs after lunch. Greig, however, was pulled by Lloyd for a spectacular six which carried high into the top tier of the Errol De Santos Stand and took Lloyd to his fifty. Did Denness consider changing his bowling? Perish the thought for in the next twenty minutes the remarkable Greig transformed the match.

The fall of Lloyd in the following over began one of those totally unexpected reversals which make cricket, and especially Test cricket, the incomparable game it is. Lloyd tried to force Greig off the back foot, edged and was caught behind by Alan Knott for 52. With Rowe, Lloyd had taken the score from 122 for 2 to 224, and now he was replaced not by Kanhai but by Sobers, as the West Indies sought to confuse England by persevering with a left-hand/right-hand combination. The sight of Sobers appearing at the top of the pavilion steps was the signal for a rumbling roar from the crowd, which today was around twenty thousand. Almost to a man they rose to clap the great man as he walked to the wicket in what in all probability was to be his final Test. With a beaming smile Sobers acknowledged also the greetings of the England close fielders. One of them, Jack Birkenshaw, helped to roll up one of his sleeves which had unfurled during his walk to the wicket. He need hardly have bothered. To his third ball Sobers played forward and there again was

125

Birkenshaw in the gully, catching the ball in both hands off the outside edge. 224 for 4, and rapturous applause was replaced by confused chatter.

Meanwhile Lawrence Rowe was hovering calmly in the nineties, pinned down by Underwood's phenomenal accuracy. Three times he swept against the spin and three times superb ground fielding by Greig at short fine leg prevented probable fours. He could not, would not be denied a place in the centre of the stage. In his next over Kanhai, who had made two, tried to drive without getting to the pitch of the ball and Greig followed through to take the return catch. 226 for 5. Another miserly over from Underwood to Rowe followed and then Murray was also out as he too drove into the air and was caught by Pocock: a nicely judged catch at extra-cover. Four wickets had fallen for eight runs and in 19 balls Greig had taken 4 for 6.

When at last the impassive Rowe, who had watched all this with the mild interest of a weekend gardener inspecting his herbaceous border, reached his third century of the series, the enormous roar from the stands must have echoed throughout the length and breadth of Trinidad. His runs had not come easily against good bowling on an increasingly tricky pitch. His third hundred of the series was a measure of his great skill, if not of his technical correctness, for time and again he had cut the ball at the last possible moment off his stumps and dextrously steered it wide of slip.

The breathless course of events was slowed a little now as Bernard Julien offered Rowe more solid support. Yet only an error by Knott, who in his excitement forgot to get behind the wicket and fumbled a fine return throw by Amiss, prevented Julien from being run out when he had made eight. He added seven further runs and had put on 38 with Rowe when he too was out to Greig, caught by Birkenshaw at backward short-leg. This was the classic off-spinner's wicket in the leg trap, of the kind that Jim Laker used to capture regularly in his halcyon years in the 1950s. By tea West Indies had been reduced to 276 for 7, a lead of only nine, and the game had been transformed.

A further April shower (in the West Indies they call it 'woman rain' — drizzle which nags away without getting to the point) held up play for twenty-five minutes after tea and for a time the crowd were delighted by the quiet artistry of Rowe and the bludgeoning aggression of Keith Boyce. The latter's massive legside heaves threatened more than they achieved and when he had made 19 he hit Greig high to deep mid-off where Pocock, who incidentally delights in walloping steepling catches for his colleagues during fielding practices, took the catch safely. The total was 300, and the very next ball, ironically a full-toss, Rowe hit straight to Boycott at mid-wicket.

Inshan Ali made five before Greig persuaded umpire Sang Hue to give one of his rare l.b.w.'s, and it was all over. The West Indian lead was only 38 and Greig had taken 8 wickets for 53 runs in the day, 8 for 86 overall, and in fourteen overs after first breaking through 8 for 38. It was the first time an England bowler had taken eight wickets in an innings against the West Indies. The feat had been achieved with a bowling method Greig had never tried in Test Matches before this tour: slow-medium off-breaks bowled from a full run-up identical to his seam bowler's approach. Moreover he had all the time been rubbing away the skin of a painfully sore spinning finger. The last time that he had had such success with this method of bowling was as a schoolboy when he had taken seven wickets on a wet wicket in an Inter-Provincial Schools Trial in South Africa. Now he had scythed away the strongest batting array in the world. It almost defied belief. Almost, but not quite, because Greig is a cricketer who believes that nothing is impossible — and he had just proved it.

With little fuss or bother Geoff Boycott and Dennis Amiss made 23 runs in the last 40 minutes of the third day and began the fourth with England only 15 runs behind. England's collapse in the second innings of the first Test at Port of Spain two months before had been the cause of their seven-wicket defeat. Now a batting side which had often failed since knew that it was facing the final and decisive challenge.

The tense progress of the match and the concentration of the players were interrupted by a succession of English-style April showers. Before tea only two hours' play was possible and in that timeEngland travelled from 23 for no wicket to 88 for 2. There was a fortuitous element for the West Indies in the taking of both wickets, but they were important ones nonetheless. Amiss and Boycott soon established themselves again against the spin of Gibbs and Sobers. A fine late-cut by Boycott took England into the lead and Amiss was playing with all the positive assurance which had marked his batting during the series. 47 runs in this innings would have taken him past Patsy Hendren's record aggregate in a series against the West Indies, but when he had made 16 he was to fall in a surprising manner.

Kanhai brought on Clive Lloyd for what seemed likely to be one exploratory over to enable Gibbs to switch to the pavilion end. But with his fifth ball Lloyd produced a virtual shooter and Amiss, for once served ill by his high backlift, could not get down to play the ball in time. He lost his off-stump and departed to the pavilion and a few comforting puffs at his favourite pipe. It would not have entered his mind – for there are few more selfless cricketers – but he could certainly have been forgiven for thinking that it was someone else's turn to withstand the pressure in the middle.

For a while another England collapse was on the cards. After Denness had hit his first four and, as it turned out, his only scoring shot, the first of several showers held up play for twenty minutes. When the action began again Boycott turned a ball wide of Kallicharran at short fine leg. Denness called for a perfectly possible quick run, as was his right with a ball played behind the wicket. He was already fatally committed by the time Boycott sent him back. Kallicharran threw to the striker's end, but Murray's lobbed throw just beat Denness to the other end. For him it was a personal tragedy and a mocking echo of his dismissal from a throw by Kallicharran in the second innings of the first Test. Moreover England were only six runs on with two good wickets down, and when Fletcher began he looked for some time about as comfortable as a man on a bed of nails.

Before he had scored Fletcher was missed by Lloyd at silly mid-off, a hard reflex chance waist high from a full-blooded drive. The suffering bowler was Inshan Ali, but though he bowled excellently and on this occasion inexpensively he was to take only one wicket in the innings. The inevitable conclusion is that only on a really quick pitch which also turns will he trouble the best Test players. Perhaps the Australian wickets would suit him?

Forty-five more minutes were lost after lunch because of another shower, but after a frustrating delay Boycott reached his second fifty of the match after 149 minutes of disciplined batting. Then, just when Fletcher was starting to settle in, yet another downpour sent the players scurrying for shelter and an early tea. The final session of play remained mercifully unmolested by the clouds and Boycott and Fletcher once again began the process of playing themselves in. Time was now becoming a serious factor for the first time, and Kanhai showed that he was not unaware of this by using Julien to a defensive field at one end while Gibbs wheeled away at the other. But this was not a pitch made for Gibbs, who likes to get his wickets with the guiles of flight and changing pace. Tony

Greig had certainly got greater turn and bounce from the pitch.

England's score gradually climbed upwards, but progress was slow until after 87 overs Kanhai called for the new ball. As so often happens, though the over-rate slackened, the scoring rate accelerated. Both Boycott and Fletcher took fours through the covers off short balls, but Fletcher, after receiving several short ones from Boyce in the same over, suddenly walked rather self-consciously up the pitch and asked Sang Hue if he were aware of the law relating to intimidatory bowling. The reply was classic: 'Out here we don't consider those balls bouncers, we consider them long-hops.' If the truth be told, that is just what most of Boyce's deliveries (on this occasion at least) were. In a county match Fletcher might not have thought twice about smacking them to mid-wicket for four. He survived the barrage such as it was, and took the partnership with Boycott past 100 only to fall at last to a superb ball from Julien. It moved in late off the seam, kept a little low, and took Fletcher's middle stump.

Pocock was sent in as night-watchman, a responsibility he thoroughly relished, and with Boycott producing one more resounding square-cut for four off Julien the day ended with England 157 for 3. Boycott was 81 not out, and though time was running out he had seen England through the crisis into a position from which they could attack again.

But fortunes in this match had shifted as suddenly as clouds on an April day, and by lunchtime on the fourth day it was the West Indies who were back in control. This was so despite another fine performance by Boycott. Until now caution had been his watchword, but from the start of the day he showed that he recognised the urgency of the situation and his batting looked all the better for it. He hit the still new ball away off his legs and through the covers with solid assurance and at last there was about his

The uninhibited enthusiasm of West Indian crowds is an integral part of the Caribbean game. *Above* A Trinidadian spectator salutes Kallicharran's century in the first Test. Amiss, perhaps, plans revenge (Julien is the other batsman). *Below* The crowd at Queen's Park Oval, Port of Spain—transistor radio to the fore. *Overleaf* Queen's Park Oval, scene of the only two decisive results in the series.

Above Weekend cricket in Barbados—makeshift props but elegant style. *Below* Rain stops play in Bridgetown—an all-too familiar occurrence during the MCC tour.

batting the timing of a man in form. But who would stay with him? Not Pocock, who was caught at mid-on as he checked an attempted drive. Not Greig, who tried to run before he could walk and turned a ball from Julien off his toes straight to square-leg. Not even Frank Hayes, who at the final time of asking could not add to his bitterly disappointing series aggregate of 60, and was trapped l.b.w. by Julien's off-cutter. Effectively, England were now 138 for 6.

At last, with a firm, well-timed on-drive off Boyce for his tenth four, Boycott reached his first hundred in eight Tests in a row against the West Indies. For him, after so many setbacks, it was a moment of sweet revenge. As for the West Indies bowlers, they must have mused that this moment had to come sometime: Boycott may have won this battle, but they had won the war. His century had taken 336 minutes to compile; it was faster by 52 minutes than his first-innings 99, yet faster also by 52 minutes than Rowe's hundred for West Indies. On a pitch which did not encourage free strokeplay but most certainly encouraged the spinners, he had used all his concentration, all his experience and all his technical know-how.

After an hour, however, England had added only 28 runs for the loss of three wickets and when Julien came off after nearly an hour and a half he had bowled nine overs for nine runs and two wickets. Alan Knott was forced by the situation to play a purely passive role at first, but he gradually worked out the pace of the pitch and its tendency to bounce at uneven heights and went into lunch with Boycott with the total advanced to 213 for 6. Then, immediately after lunch, Lance Gibbs struck the crucial blow.

His first ball to Boycott was well pitched up, just outside the off stump. Boycott met it, as he had met countless similar balls, with a defensive forward stroke. This time, however, he played over the top of the ball, and the impregnable defence was broken at last. Or was it? The bails were on the ground, Murray was clapping, and the obvious assumption was that Boycott had been bowled. But Boycott stood his ground, believing firmly that the ball had rebounded off the wicket-keeper's pads onto the stumps. Umpire Sang Hue at the bowler's end had been unsighted by the batsman and looked to his colleague Stewart Ishmael, who gave a nod of the head to confirm that, as far as he was concerned, the bails had gone backwards and Boycott had been bowled for 112. He departed to boos when he well deserved cheers,and with him went England's hopes of a score of around 300.

Jack Birkenshaw made 7 before, as in the first innings, he was caught in the gully. This time it was a ball from a slow bowler, Inshan Ali, which popped and spun off the shoulder of the bat. Again his departure left all the onus on Alan Knott, who was busily picking up runs in singles but was unable to wrest back the initiative. Geoff Arnold, who has no inhibitions when it comes to batting, offered a sensible straight bat to the spinners and added a valuable 38 runs with Knott before he was yorked by Gary Sobers's 'arm' ball. Underwood, too, looked as though he could fend for himself for a while, but he did not get the chance to prove it for when Knott had made 44 he swung across a full-toss from Sobers and was given out l.b.w. by umpire Ishmael to a ball which many observers thought he had hit. Both Knott and Underwood clearly thought the decision was wrong, but it had been made and that was that. Knott was no doubt much too disappointed to reflect that at least he had just become (in all probability) the final victim in Sobers's Test career. It seemed of much greater significance that England were all out for 263 and that West Indies needed to score 226 on a tired pitch to win the match and the series.

The final conflict was postponed. After forty minutes' batting and ten overs a heavy tropical downpour ended play for the day. In this time West Indies made an important and assertive move towards their target, Rowe and Fredericks scoring 30 without being parted, though not without several moments of fortune. Both went for their strokes as England opened with Arnold's seamers and Greig's off-cutters. For a time, as the storm approached, the atmosphere was unpleasantly oppressive, but Arnold was unable to find the length which might have enabled him to swing the ball disconcertingly. It was Greig, from the pavilion end, whose bounce and spin beat Fredericks more than once. Twice he and Knott appealed for l.b.w., the second time so vehemently that if looks could kill umpire Ishmael would have been forced to wing his way to what verbose cricket obituary writers sometimes call the 'great pavilion in the sky'. As it was, umpires, batsmen and bowlers alike were soon sprinting for the cover of a terrestrial haven, and the last two hours of the day were lost.

In the rum-shops of the Caribbean and the distant public bars of Britain the arguments that night were fierce and intense. 196 runs for such a batting side: surely it was a cakewalk? But what about that Trinidad pitch? And what about Tony Greig? Rowe and Fredericks were in form alright, but Kanhai wasn't, Sobers wasn't, even Kallicharran and Lloyd were not. Even now, either side could win and a Port of Spain taxi-driver summed it up in good Trinidadian terms: 'Listen man, dat game gonna be close. I'm telling you. It's gonna be real close, man.'

And it was. Unbearably close. The morning was mercifully sunny as play began at ten o'clock before a sparse crowd. The ground soon filled up, though. Trinidadians are notoriously late for everything, and in any case the radios all over Port of Spain soon had spectators hurrying towards the Queen's Park Oval as news of the progress of the match spread. At first it was all good news for West Indies.

Denness opened not with Greig but with Pocock and Underwood and again Rowe and Fredericks were quick to take advantage of anything like a loose delivery. Underwood was right on the spot at once, bowling four overs for four runs before Greig came on in his place at the pavilion end. But Pocock, though he turned the occasional ball sharply, strayed at times down the leg-side where Fredericks is so strong. When he had made 22, however, Fredericks tried to force Pocock off the back foot and nicked the ball straight to Fletcher at slip.It was a sharp, straight chance and it went down. Would this be the pattern of the day? English frustration, and a gradual inexorable march towards a West Indian victory?

33 runs had been added without an English success when a wave of the arms from Douglas Sang Hue signalled the wheeling on of the water cart and the end of the first hour's conflict. The first over afterwards was bowled by Jack Birkenshaw and at last the breakthrough came. Rowe went back to a ball which came sharply back from the off and with his pads almost back on the stumps as the ball struck them Sang Hue had no hesitation in responding to Birkenshaw's triumphant bark by lifting the finger of judgment. There was something especially pleasing about the fact that it should have been Birkenshaw who had taken this vital wicket. It is a fair guess that no one received a more glowing tour report than this loyal team man, and his timely blow triggered off a heartening performance in which England truly played as a team. They knew that the memory of all the setbacks and disappointments of the early part of the tour could be wiped out if things went right on this final day. And now it was the West Indies' turn to subside before the pressure.

Kallicharran played one defensive stroke to Birkenshaw, then faced his second ball from Greig. He went forward, got an outside edge and Fletcher at slip took the catch off Knott's body. 64 for 2 and as Kallicharran walked back after collecting his first Test pair, he must have thought ruefully of the time two months before when his innings of 158 had helped West Indies to win the first Test Match and had made him the hero of Trinidad. What a humbling game is cricket!

Fate had a more severe blow for West Indies only just round the corner. In the next over Roy Fredericks flicked a ball from Birkenshaw past Boycott at mid-wicket. It was a comfortable single, a dangerous two. Lloyd saw the danger, tried to send Fredericks back, and both then watched in horror as Boycott's perfect throw came whistling over the top of the stumps and Knott took off the bails with both batsmen stranded in the middle of the pitch. Fredericks was the closer to Knott and it was he who had to go. 65 for 3; and once again this pulsating Test Match had taken a swift, dramatic turn.

Kanhai and Lloyd took the score to 69 before there was a ten-minute hold-up for one of those fitful Trinidadian showers and then Lloyd suddenly moved into action with three resounding fours in succession off Birkenshaw – a straight drive and two well-timed sweeps. The crowd, now large and excited, leapt and shrieked. Suddenly that target of 226 seemed very close again. But Kanhai, a man who no longer seemed to relish a crisis and whose great talents were on the wane, rashly chased a wide ball from Greig down the off-side and snicked it to Fletcher. So at 84 for 4 Gary Sobers came out to play what in all probability was to be his final Test innings. There were just seven minutes to go till lunch, and in that time Greig produced his *coup de grâce* – for the morning, at least. He bowled a ball of tempting flight to Lloyd, who drove without getting to the pitch and lifted the ball well to the off side of the wicket. (Lloyd, of course, is a left-hander.) Greig, following through, first had to change direction, then with three enormous strides he was across the pitch and diving to hold the ball in a telescopic right arm. It was simply miraculous and of the twenty-two men in the match only Lloyd himself could have taken such a catch. But Lloyd's part in the game was ended. West Indies were 89 for 5 at lunch and heading for a humiliating defeat.

Now the length and strength of the West Indies batting order was underlined. Sobers and Murray each began the afternoon without a run to his name, but Sobers, who so often in his glorious past had rescued the West Indies from apparently hopeless situations, began to play some of those easy, graceful classical strokes which had established him as one of modern cricket's most elegant stylists as well as its supreme player. Soon the crowd and the scoreboard were alive again. Murray played equally well; he has always had a calm head in a crisis and it was one of several good forcing strokes by him past cover which brought the target inside a hundred.

Sobers, when 19, escaped a chance to Fletcher at slip off the unfortunate Pocock, but the fifty partnership soon followed and those optimistic West Indians who had said at lunchtime 'We will win by five wickets just before tea' were smiling happily. The average West Indian cricket-follower tends to be dogmatic and a trifle arrogant in his cricketing judgments. But anyone who dared to make confident predictions about this match deserved to be humbled and those who did were soon seen to have been whistling in the dark.

Not before time Derek Underwood was brought back into the attack from the northern end and when the score had reached 135 he had his supreme moment of the tour. After pinning Sobers forward with those flat, mean, accurate deliveries in which he specialises, Underwood (the man some say is unable to flight the ball) at last gave a ball a tempting extra foot or two of air. Sobers lunged forward to drive, swirled at thin air, and was bowled. It was the crucial wicket and the more sweet for Underwood for the fact that Sobers in his time had often punished him severely. Indeed this was only the second time he had ever dismissed Sobers in a Test Match. No wonder Underwood ran down the wicket to meet Alan Knott and no wonder the little man seized him by the waist and lifted him clean off the ground! Not that the game was over yet, for Julien and Boyce were still to come. Julien had enjoyed a very good series, but now he played a thoroughly irresponsible shot, trying to hit Greig over the top before he had settled and presenting Denness at extra-cover with a simple catch.

In came the belligerent figure of Boyce, and soon he had the crowd massed thickly in the top tier of the Carib Beer Stand leaping and dancing again as he swept Greig for four, first one side of fine leg, then the other. In less time, it seemed, than it takes to tell he had scored 18, all his runs coming behind square on the leg-side. In between, however, his defence was solid, and Murray was still there at the other end. If these two could have stayed together until tea there would still have been a chance for the West Indies to make up for their earlier carelessness, for the wicket was no more venomous now than it had been since the deadening effects of the roller had worn off after the first hour. Indeed Greig, the game's hero now whether England won or lost, was certainly tiring, and his spinning finger was becoming painfully sore again. But he now produced one more decisive blow. His penultimate ball before tea was well wide of the off-stump, well pitched up and given plenty of air. Murray, who had been mindful of the need to keep the scoreboard ticking along from the start of his innings, decided to go for an off-drive. But like so many others in the match he was deceived by some late dip in the flight, achieved in Greig's case not by a Gibbsian ability to make the ball float and hold up suddenly in the air but probably by the very height of his delivery. Perhaps it is something which batsmen will grow used to; perhaps he will never have such outstanding success again. That lies in the future, though. To this ball Murray did not quite get to the pitch and could only edge it to Fletcher, who took his third catch of the day at slip.

So at tea the West Indies had been reduced to 166 for 8, and their only hope now seemed to be for Boyce to change his approach and, with a few of those whirlwind swings which have changed the course of many a one-day match in favour of his adopted county Essex, try to turn this crucial Test Match too. In the event a stand for the ninth wicket did indeed develop; yet its hero was not Boyce but Inshan Ali. The little left-hander was certainly under-estimated by England; with a sound and well-organised technique and a sensible approach he picked up runs as they were offered in one's and two's. If Denness made any mistake on this last day it was perhaps in not applying sufficient pressure at this stage. Runs began to flow far too easily for English comfort and each one was applauded with increasing volume and excitement by a crowd far less cool and composed than their own special favourite Inshan. At 188, with only 38 runs needed,he made his first mistake, turning a ball into and out of the hands of Frank Hayes at forward short-leg. Hayes was moving forward, anticipating the catch, and this was why he dropped what might have been a crucial chance.

At 194, with just 30 to win and two wickets standing, Denness took the brave decision to summon the new ball. 'England are beaten' was the immediate reaction of one experienced commentator. (Off mike, fortunately for him!) Certainly the taking of the new ball was no clearcut decision. It had been available for several overs, but spin it was which had done all the damage and the danger was that two well-set batsmen would find the ball coming on to them even more easily. Arnold's first over of the day was without venom, and Inshan played it like a master. A West Indian yelled out my name near the commentary box, and when I looked out he slid his finger across his throat with a confident smile. The feeling was growing around the ground. Perhaps England *were* beaten. Greig continued with the new ball from the pavilion end, still bowling his off-breaks, and suddenly, for no particular reason except the general one of inexperience, Inshan tried to loft a ball on his off-stump. His drive came off the middle of the bat but it curled away in the air towards Derek Underwood at deep mid-off. Many a similar catch has been dropped in moments of great tension like this one. But Underwood caught the ball safely in front of his chest, threw it high into the air and a ninth-wicket partnership worth 31 runs was over.

Twenty-nine runs were still needed when Lance Gibbs, cricket's most experienced last man in, and of all members of the union of number eleven batsmen the least likely to play like anything else, came into face the inevitable. Keith Boyce was 33 not out by now and had played exceptionally well in a brave attempt to make up for the failures of the front-line batsmen earlier in the day. He knew the capabilities of Gibbs as well as anyone and (though it is easy to dole out the blame from the boundary and desperately hard to think rationally in the heat of a tense finish to a crucial game) he was at fault now in making no effort to protect his partner. With Gibbs at the wicket, the new ball was a positive advantage to England and once he was exposed to Arnold it was just a matter of time before the end. At five minutes past four, in the first of the mandatory last twenty overs of the day, a straight fast ball found a direct route to the leg-stump past a blind flail of Gibbs's bat and it was all over.

England had won by 26 runs a match which for sustained tension, frequent and swift changes of fortune and its pulsating finish will go down as one of the great Tests. They thus squared a series which everyone had expected them to lose and which but for several pieces of individual heroism they must indeed have lost. Their final hero was Tony Greig. On this last day he had taken 5 for 70 to finish with thirteen wickets in the match for 156, so becoming the first Englishman since Jim Laker in 1956 to take more than twelve wickets in a Test Match. In four Tests with his off-breaks he had taken 24 wickets. The West Indies could blame themselves to a large extent for failing to get those 196 runs on the last day. At the crunch, England's icy professionalism had overcome the more fitful talents of the West Indies and Boycott's dedicated batting and Greig's brilliant bowling had been decisive. But the events of the match in general and the final day in particular were aptly summed up by a question from a small boy playing cricket on the outfield an hour after the game had ended. 'Listen, mister', he pleaded. 'How *could* West Indies lose that game?' I did not know how to answer him.

9

Analysis of a Daylight Robbery

After nine long years the West Indies were still without a win in a Test series at home. It was strange that while MCC were enjoying a gentle ending to the tour with a couple of matches in Bermuda, West Indians were analysing a failure and England a belated but nonetheless welcome success. England's recovery, starting with their sudden improvement in Guyana, had been the result of hard work and determination. They were thus able to prove that they were not as bad a side as they appeared to be in the early part of the tour – nor as dispirited a team as they had just occasionally seemed. But their brave and honourable finish to the tour and their win on merit in the final Test did not alter the belief that to have earned a half share in a series dominated by the West Indies was something like daylight robbery.

In their disappointment West Indian cricket officials could console themselves that they now had one of the best teams in their history, and that with faster wickets they might not just have won the series but won it easily. In the second and third Tests England were forced by the situation they found themselves in to play defensive cricket, and the slowness and unresponsiveness of the pitches at Sabina Park and Bridgetown made defeat of a side intent only on survival a very difficult task. Of course, had the matches been played on faster pitches West Indies might not have built up the dominating positions they did in these games and England's faster bowlers might have had more success. But the frailty of England's batting against the fast bowlers suggests that the West Indies

141

would have benefited more than England from quicker wickets, and England's performance on a very fast wicket at Lord's the previous summer suggested this too. Somehow West Indian groundsmen will have to find a way of putting back some pace into their wickets. It was not so long ago that Wes Hall retired and they were talking in the Caribbean of 'pace like fire'. For all his herculean efforts, the pace of Keith Boyce was more often like a damp squib, and after the first Test poor Bob Willis hardly ever passed the bat at all.

There was less cause for the West Indies players to reproach themselves, although like England many times in the past they must have been disgusted that they had only been able to draw a series they should have won. Never indeed had an outstanding Test team, as this by any standards certainly was, had such a brief period at peak performance. For with Gary Sobers not being available for the 1974—5 tour of India, and no Test series in the West Indies until 1976, the chances were that the peerless all-rounder has played his final Test. In addition, Rohan Kanhai lost the captaincy to Clive Lloyd after a reign spanning only thirteen Tests, and the other great Guyanese veteran, Lance Gibbs, was clearly nearing the end of his career. It was the special blend of the ripe skills of these three, the maturity of Fredericks, Lloyd, Murray and Boyce, and the burgeoning genius of Rowe, Kallicharran and Julien which made the team as a whole such a formidable mixture. The batting was immensely strong. Only twice in the series did they need to have a second innings and such was the depth of the batting that not until it happened in the last Test did anyone really believe that England would be capable of bowling them out twice. That they did so does not alter the potential strength of a batting order which a judge as knowledgeable as Trevor Bailey, who played against the three W's at their peak, believes to be the best the West

Indies have produced.

Throughout the series the fielding of the West Indies side was something to be marvelled at. Often in the past West Indies have thrown away vital chances in the field and tended to get ragged when things have started to go against them. England were not able very often to put pressure on the West Indies to test this theory, but one very good reason for this was the wonderful consistency of the fielding and the brilliance of much of the catching. The pressure, indeed, always seemed to be on England. In the outfield Boyce must be one of the hardest throwers of all time – and one of the longest. More than once he rifled the ball for overthrows through or wide of Murray's gloves and on past fielders anxious to preserve the bones in their hands. In addition Kallicharran and Julien are superbly accurate throwers with returns so flat and fast that even if they have to pursue the ball to the boundary two runs rather than three are all the batsmen dare run. (Denness and Amiss tried to run a third to Kallicharran in the first Test with fatal and far-reaching consequences.) At cover or anywhere else Clive Lloyd is simply the most talented fielder in the world. Those long-devouring strides, those elastic arms, that marvellous sense of anticipation, the amazing speed with which he can move into the throw almost in the same instant as he picks up the ball, and the magnetic accuracy of the throw itself all contrive to make him a constant menace to the unwary batsman. If he had not made a run in the series (and he made only 147 in all) Lloyd would have been almost worth a place for his fielding alone. He achieved three single-handed run-outs and saved countless runs at other times.

Close to the wicket, Roy Fredericks took ten fine catches and revealed lightning reactions; Rowe and Kanhai were safe; and only Sobers, rather surprisingly, let the side down. Murray, who missed practically nothing that mattered, completed a formidable unit.

When the side is compared with other great Test teams, it can be faulted only for the lack of penetration of its bowling. This seems rather a harsh thing to say, perhaps, about a team which at one stage seemed to have its opponents in an almost permanent state of collapse, but in the second and third Test Matches the bowlers were unable to finish the job they had begun. Nevertheless this was a more than useful attack, with a wonderful variety. Boyce could be genuinely fast, and, more than that, unpleasantly hostile. Most of his eleven wickets came from dangerous bounce or from sheer speed, because he hardly ever moved a ball through the air or off the seam. Julien, his regular opening partner, bowled increasingly well and could always be relied on to trouble batsmen with his movement off the pitch or occasionally with dangerous late swing. Sobers too bowled well, five of his fourteen wickets coming from his faster style, the rest – including the decisive spell of three wickets in fifteen balls in the first Test – with his orthodox left-arm spinners.

Of the other spinners, Gibbs, of course, was out-standing. His subtle variations and skilful flight were a joy to watch and a menace to play against, as his figures testify. In addition to these four main bowlers, Fredericks and Lloyd could always be called on for a useful spell and at different times in the series the leg-spinner Barrett, the left-arm back-of-the-hand spinner Inshan Ali, and the promising fast bowler Roberts all did well. Only Vanburn Holder was disappointing, though he played in only one Test and was the man mainly responsible for inflicting the heaviest and most humiliating defeat of the tour – the ten-wicket victory by Barbados.

The superb batting of Alvin Kallicharran in the first three Tests (until England exposed what may be only a temporary weakness against off-spin) and the arrival of Lawrence Rowe as a great batsman perhaps gave West Indians cause for greatest satisfaction. Rowe, an impassive, taciturn figure who once used to whistle while he batted to show his supreme indifference to the bowlers, was the outstanding player in an exceptional batting side. With his 302 at Bridgetown he finally silenced those who said he could not play well outside Sabina Park, and joined the select company of nine others who have scored a triple hundred in a Test. In the final Test at Trinidad he played Tony Greig and the other England spinners much better than anyone else. Such is his commitment to the back foot that his ability to make runs consistently on faster or greener pitches will remain in doubt until he proves otherwise, but there is a mercenary remorselessness and an easy balance about his run-gathering which suggests that he will be no nine-day wonder.

England had less reason to be pleased with the tour as a whole, or to be complacent about the future. Only two men came home with their reputations enhanced. But these two, Dennis Amiss and Tony Greig, were so out-standing that they enabled England to save the second and third Tests and to win the fifth. Amiss, whose 262 not out was one of those great pieces of individual heroism which Test cricket sometimes inspires, had a Test aggregate of 663 runs, only narrowly missing Patsy Hendren's record, and he became only the fifth English player to score over 1000 runs in the Caribbean. Apart from slightly longer hair, the Amiss who left England in January was the same as the Amiss who came home in April. As a batsman the change was one not of style or technique but of confidence. Even in the sad nervous early days of his Test career Amiss had looked a player of great ability. Now he had proved the point, to his own satisfaction and everyone else's.

It was a nice irony that Tony Greig, after being under a cloud in the first Test, should have ended the series as the man considered most likely and (of this team) best equipped to lead England in Australia. Having expressed his apologies for his part in the unhappy situation at Port of Spain, he put the whole business out of his mind and settled down to play an outstanding series, scoring centuries in successive Tests, developing a devastating new method of bowling and holding some superb catches. Behind all that he did was the intensely competitive spirit of one of the bravest and most determined of all modern players. In the third Test at Bridgetown in particular it seemed that for hour after hour only his refusal to yield an inch stood between the West Indies and victory. In that match he became the first England player to score a century and take five wickets in a Test innings. Then, in Port of Spain, his record figures of 13 for 156 saved the series for England.

Greig had first used these medium-slow off-breaks as a schoolboy in South Africa when in a Nuffield Inter-Provincial trial he had once taken seven wickets in an innings on a wet wicket. After taking no wickets with his seamers in the first Test, his inventive cricket brain told him that the slow, gently turning wickets of the Caribbean might be better suited to his spinners and suddenly England found that they too had a Gary Sobers who could turn from one style to another without loss of control. How superbly he bowled in the last three Test Matches and what a difference he made to the England side! Perhaps batsmen will find a method of counteracting his spin and unusual flight once the novelty wears off, but on helpful wickets his bounce alone is sure to make him a dangerous bowler. His success with this method was the biggest gain of all on the tour, because the scarcity – indeed almost total non-existence of good young off-spinners in England – remains with the lack of middle-order batsmen the most pressing problem.

When he was not batting or bowling (which was not very often) Greig was usually finding some way to entertain the crowd. Like the Indian crowds in the previous winter, Caribbean spectators were fascinated by this enthusiastic giraffe. They laughed when first they saw his eccentric high stance and again when ball after ball he would throw his arms high in the air as if it was only an act of God which had enabled the batsman to play the ball with the middle of the bat and thus prevent him from taking another wicket. Whether he fielded in the hip pocket of the batsman at silly-point or patrolled the boundary fence, the spectators loved the antics he produced to entertain them, obvious though they sometimes seemed. They loved too the towering sixes he occasionally produced with an easy swing of a bat propelled by immensely strong arm and back muscles. In short, Greig was an entertainer, and though he sometimes became the abused villain of the crowd with his occasional tendency to excessive and overt gamesmanship, he was much more often an appreciated clown. In a team short of 'characters', if not of character, Greig stood out like a colossus. The England team seems sure to be built around his massive presence for many years.

What sort of team will it be, and who will be its captain? The verdict on Mike Denness at the end of his first tour of leadership must be that he was saved largely by individual heroics. It should not be forgotten that he began the tour on a hiding to nothing and that he hardly put a foot wrong in the last two Tests. He was unable to carry his side along with him fully in the early part of the tour, and some of the players lost confidence in him, but when he realised that his independent style of detached leadership was not working he made big efforts to become a more approachable figure and improved all the time as a controller of events on the field. The real problem is that though he is an excellent player of moderate bowling, he did not look on the evidence of this tour to be a good enough player against top-class fast bowling to be a consistently high scorer in Tests. A frail batting side cannot afford to include anyone not strictly worth his place.

Of course, Denness was not the only batting failure. The

unfortunate Frank Hayes, after beginning his Test career with a century, could make only 60 runs in seven innings and totally lost his confidence. He should console himself by remembering that a certain Dennis Amiss also once looked as though he would not have the temperament to succeed in Test cricket.

John Jameson, an excellent team man and a cheerful soul, was equally disappointing because he consistently tried to run before he could walk. At least he played some good, beefy innings outside the Tests and when asked to bowl he did so with some success.

Keith Fletcher, despite his excellent second-innings hundred at Bridgetown, continued to waste much of his considerable talent because of his nervousness and un-certainty at the start of an innings. He remains something of an enigma and as an experienced Test cricketer it is time he started to play more often with the confidence and authority of one.

By his own high standards Geoff Boycott was dis-appointing too. His single-minded and wonderfully sound batting in the final Test had much to do with England's win and did much also to re-establish his reputation. But not until he returns to Australia will we know for sure how permanent was the damage done to his batting by the devastating fast bowling of Dennis Lillee in England in 1972. The chances are that he will work out his problems in his own dedicated way and that the years between 1972 and 1974 will in time be looked on as simply a lean period in a great career.

In the second half of the tour Alan Knott re-established his reputation as a batsman of high class and particularly as a skilful player of spin bowling, after his long period without a big Test innings. His return to form made a big difference to the side. But his wicket-keeping was not at its best and his cheerful understudy Bob Taylor, who kept immaculately when given the chance, was certainly the most unfortunate member of the touring party.

England's batting failures generally were no surprise – they had been a depressing feature of England cricket for several seasons. But the failure of the faster bowlers especially was certainly unexpected. Between them, Bob Willis, Geoff Arnold and Chris Old could earn only twelve Test wickets. For West Indies Julien took 16 and Boyce 11. When John Snow had toured West Indies in 1968 he had taken 27 Test wickets by himself, on pitches admittedly better suited to fast bowlers, and both Jeff Jones and David Brown took more wickets by themselves on that tour than Willis, Arnold and Old put together. In the Island matches Mike Hendrick at least applied himself to the basic rules of keeping an accurate line and length and he was ready by the end of the tour to step into the England side and do well.

Even the spinners were disappointing – apart, of course, from Greig. Pat Pocock remains a dangerous bowler who turns the ball as much as any off-spinner, but a lack of perfect control meant that his nine Test wickets were expensively gained at 61 runs each. Derek Underwood, though he really found his form again at the end of the tour, was also expensive overall in terms of runs per wicket, but after an unfortunate injury Jack Birkenshaw served his side well in the last few weeks.

A great many English disappointments were washed away by the glory and excitement of the final Test, but it was the West Indies who contributed more overall to a series which, with two tense draws and two matches ending in pulsating final-day victories, will never be forgotten by those who followed it.

MCC in the West Indies 1973-74

A statistical survey compiled by Bill Frindall

1 The Teams

The MCC touring team to the West Indies and Bermuda

Players	County	Age on 1 Jan 74
DENNESS, Michael Henry (Captain)	Kent	33
AMISS, Dennis Leslie	Warwickshire	30
ARNOLD, Geoffrey Graham	Surrey	29
BIRKENSHAW, Jack	Leicestershire	33
BOYCOTT, Geoffrey	Yorkshire	33
FLETCHER, Keith William Robert	Essex	29
GREIG, Anthony William (Vice-captain)	Sussex	27
HAYES, Frank Charles	Lancashire	27
HENDRICK, Michael	Derbyshire	25
JAMESON, John Alexander	Warwickshire	32
KNOTT, Alan Philip Eric	Kent	27
OLD, Christopher Middleton	Yorkshire	25
POCOCK, Patrick Ian	Surrey	27
TAYLOR, Robert William	Derbyshire	32
UNDERWOOD, Derek Leslie	Kent	28
WILLIS, Robert George Dylan	Warwickshire	24

Manager

CARR, Donald Bryce	Secretary, T.C.C.B. (Ex-Derbyshire)	47

Their West Indies opponents

Players	Country	Age on 1 Jan 74
KANHAI, Rohan Babulal (Captain)	Guyana	38
ALI, Inshan	Trinidad	24
BARRETT, Arthur George	Jamaica	31
BOYCE, Keith David	Barbados	30
FOSTER, Maurice Linton Churchill	Jamaica	30
FREDERICKS, Roy Clifton	Guyana	31
GIBBS, Lancelot Richard (Vice-captain)	Guyana	39
HOLDER, Vanburn Alonza	Barbados	28
JULIEN, Bernard Denis	Trinidad	23
KALLICHARRAN, Alvin Isaac	Guyana	24
LLOYD, Clive Hubert	Guyana	29
MURRAY, Deryck Lance	Trinidad	30
ROBERTS, Anderson Montgomery Everton	Antigua	22
ROWE, Lawrence George	Jamaica	24
SOBERS, Garfield St Aubrun	Barbados	37

2 The averages

All statistics are based on details extracted from the MCC Touring Team's official scorebook.

The two matches played in Bermuda after the Fifth Test are excluded from this survey but the scores can be found on pages 170–171

Match record of official MCC teams in the West Indies

Season	Captain	First-class matches					All matches				
		P	W	L	D	T	P	W	L	D	T
1910-11	A.F.Somerset	11	3	4	3	1	13	5	4	3	1
1912-13	A.F. Somerset	9	5	3	1	–	9	5	3	1	–
1925-26	Hon F.S.G.Calthorpe	12	2	1	9	–	13	2	1	10	–
1929-30	Hon F.S.G.Calthorpe	12	4	2	6	–	13	4	2	7	–
1934-35	R.E.S.Wyatt	12	2	2	8	–	12	2	2	8	–
1947-48	G.O.B.Allen	11	0	2	9	–	11	0	2	9	–
1953-54	L.Hutton	10	6	2	2	–	14	7	2	5	–
1959-60	P.B.H.May	13	4	1	8	–	15	4	1	10	–
1967-68	M.C.Cowdrey	12	3	0	9	–	16	4	0	12	–
1973-74	**M.H.Denness**	**11**	**1**	**2**	**8**	**–**	**14**	**2**	**3**	**9**	**–**
TOTALS		113	30	19	63	1	130	35	20	74	1

Matches abandoned without a ball being bowled are excluded.

West Indies v England – in the West Indies

Series	Tests				Bridgetown			Georgetown			Kingston			Port-of-Spain		
	P	E	WI	D	E	WI	D	E	WI	D	E	WI	D	E	WI	D
1929-30	4	1	1	2	–	–	1	–	1	–	–	–	1	1	–	–
1934-35	4	1	2	1	1	–	–	–	–	1	–	1	–	–	1	–
1947-48	4	0	2	2	–	–	1	–	1	–	–	1	–	–	–	1
1953-54	5	2	2	1	–	1	–	1	–	–	1	1	–	–	–	1
1959-60	5	1	0	4	–	–	1	–	–	1	–	–	1	1	–	1
1967-68	5	1	0	4	–	–	1	–	–	1	–	–	1	1	–	1
1973-74	**5**	**1**	**1**	**3**	**–**	**–**	**1**	**–**	**–**	**1**	**–**	**–**	**1**	**1**	**1**	**–**
TOTALS	32	7	8	17	1	1	5	1	2	4	1	3	4	4	2	4

Test match averages

England — batting and fielding

	M	I	NO	HS	Runs	Av	100	50	6s	4s	Runs/ 100B	Ct/ St
D.L.Amiss	5	9	1	262*	663	82.87	3	–	1	87	42	–
A.W.Greig	5	9	0	148	430	47.77	2	–	4	49	44	7
G.Boycott	5	9	0	112	421	46.77	1	3	–	51	30	2
A.P.E.Knott	5	9	1	87	365	45.62	–	3	1	41	39	4/-
K.W.R. Fletcher	4	7	1	129*	262	43.66	1	–	–	36	33	6
M.H. Denness	5	9	0	67	231	25.66	–	1	1	31	35	5
R.G.D. Willis	3	5	4	10*	25	25.00	–	–	–	1	18	3
J.A. Jameson	2	4	0	38	73	18.25	–	–	1	10	41	–
D.L.Underwood	4	7	3	24	67	16.75	–	–	–	9	33	2
F.C.Hayes	4	7	0	24	60	8.57	–	–	–	4	20	2
G.G.Arnold	3	5	1	13	34	8.50	–	–	–	5	19	1
P.I.Pocock	4	7	0	23	52	7.42	–	–	1	2	22	3
C.M.Old	4	7	0	19	50	7.14	–	–	1	4	23	–
J.Birkenshaw	2	3	0	8	15	5.00	–	–	–	3	35	2

England — bowling

	O	M	R	W	Av	5W/I	BB	Runs/ 100B	Balls /Wkt
A.W.Greig	207.1	46	543	24	22.62	3	8-86	44	52
R.G.D.Willis	73	15	255	5	51.00	–	3-97	58	88
P.I.Pocock	200	50	550	9	61.11	1	5-110	46	133
C.M.Old	87.4	15	313	5	62.60	–	3-89	60	105
D.L.Underwood	137.5	45	314	5	62.80	–	2-48	38	165

Also bowled: G.G.Arnold 49.3-11-148-2; J.Birkenshaw 40-9-96-2;
K.W.R.Fletcher 0.5-0-5-0; J.A.Jameson 7-2-17-1.

West Indies — batting and fielding

	M	I	NO	HS	Runs	Av	100	50	6s	4s	Runs/ 100B
L.G.Rowe	5	7	0	302	616	88.00	3	–	3	73	49
R.C.Fredericks	5	7	1	98	397	66.16	–	4	–	49	43
A.I.Kallicharran	5	7	0	158	397	56.71	2	1	1	54	45
B.D.Julien	5	5	1	86*	172	43.00	–	2	1	24	64
D.L.Murray	5	5	2	53*	113	37.66	–	1	–	7	34
K.D.Boyce	4	4	1	34*	87	29.00	–	–	2	9	73
R.B.Kanhai	5	7	1	44	157	26.16	–	–	1	21	46
C.H.Lloyd	5	7	1	52	147	24.50	–	1	3	16	42
G.St.A.Sobers	4	5	0	57	100	20.00	–	1	1	12	37
Inshan Ali	2	3	0	15	29	9.66	–	–	–	3	34
A.M.E.Roberts	1	1	1	9*	9	–	–	–	–	–	24
V.A.Holder	1	1	0	8	8	8.00	–	–	–	1	27
L.R.Gibbs	5	4	2	6*	9	4.50	–	–	–	1	23
A.G.Barrett	2	1	0	0	0	0.00	–	–	–	–	0

M.L.C.Foster played in one Test but did not bat.

West Indies — bowling

	O	M	R	W	Av	5w/I	BB	Runs/ 100B	Balls /Wkt
B.D.Julien	174	51	378	16	23.62	1	5-57	36	65
K.D.Boyce	118.4	23	324	11	29.45	–	4-42	46	65
G.St.A.Sobers	223.2	92	421	14	30.07	–	3-54	31	96
L.R.Gibbs	328	103	661	18	36.72	1	6-108	34	109
A.G.Barrett	124	46	260	7	37.14	–	3-86	35	106
Inshan Ali	113	34	248	5	49.60	–	3-86	37	136

Also bowled: M.L.C.Foster 16-5-32-0; R.C.Fredericks 34-7-93-1; V.A.Holder 42-12-105-2; A.I.Kallicharran 4-0-17-0; R.B.Kanhai 3-1-8-0; C.H.Lloyd 56-21-71-3; A.M.E.Roberts 50-12-124-3; L.G.Rowe 3-1-6-0.

First-class match averages

MCC — batting and fielding

	M	I	NO	HS	Runs	Av	100	50	6s	4s	Mins	Ct/St
D.L.Amiss	9	16	1	262*	1120	74.66	5	2	2	151	2743	3
G.Boycott	10	16	3	261*	960	73.84	3	4	2	108	2885	3
A.W.Greig	9	14	1	148	665	51.15	3	1	6	70	1577	12
K.W.R.Fletcher	10	16	3	129*	564	43.38	2	1	–	70	1715	9
M.H.Denness	10	17	2	67	504	33.60	–	4	2	61	1458	5
J.Birkenshaw	5	6	2	53*	127	31.75	–	1	1	15	297	2
F.C.Hayes	9	16	2	88	444	31.71	–	3	2	47	1318	8
R.G.D.Willis	6	6	5	10*	30	30.00	–	–	–	2	180	8
A.P.E.Knott	10	17	1	87	474	29.62	–	3	1	53	1414	14/-
J.A.Jameson	7	13	0	91	325	25.00	–	2	4	48	528	6
R.W.Taylor	3	3	0	65	69	23.00	–	1	–	10	168	5/1
M.Hendrick	5	5	3	16	29	14.50	–	–	–	6	46	2
D.L.Underwood	7	10	3	24	100	14.28	–	–	–	12	336	5
G.G.Arnold	8	10	2	25	101	12.62	–	–	1	11	352	2
C.M.Old	6	10	0	53	122	12.20	–	1	5	11	311	2
P.I.Pocock	7	11	0	23	77	7.00	–	–	1	4	370	3

MCC — bowling

	O	M	R	W	Av	5w/I	BB	Runs/100B	Balls/Wkt
A.W.Greig	277.1	57	766	30	25.53	3	8-86	46	55
M.Hendrick	108.2	21	320	12	26.66	–	4-38	49	54
J.Birkenshaw	165.5	35	467	16	29.18	1	6-101	47	62
R.G.D.Willis	140	27	526	15	35.06	–	4-91	63	56
P.I.Pocock	326.3	79	844	19	44.42	1	5-110	43	103
D.L.Underwood	263.5	88	573	12	47.75	–	3-80	36	132
G.G.Arnold	174.3	40	611	12	50.91	1	5-44	58	87
C.M.Old	135.4	28	459	9	51.00	–	3-56	56	90

Also bowled: G.Boycott 9-1-33-1; K.W.R.Fletcher 20.5-4-63-3; F.C.Hayes 0.2-0-4-0; J.A.Jameson 35-10-74-4.

3 The scores

v Combined Leeward-Windward Islands (not first-class)
1st Match
Played at Victoria Park, Castries, St Lucia, on January 16, 1974.
Toss-Combined Islands. Combined Islands won by 5 runs.
Combined Islands 204-6 in 50 overs (J.C.Allen 102 n.o.,
L.C. Sergeant 78. G.G.Arnold 3-27, C.M.Old 3-30).
MCC 199-6 in 50 overs (D.L.Amiss 114, G.Boycott 36, N. Phillip
3-41).

v Windward Islands
2nd Match
At Victoria Park, Castries, St Lucia, on January 18, 19, 20. Match
abandoned without a ball being bowled.

v Windward Islands (not first-class)
3rd Match
Played at Victoria Park, Castries, St Lucia, on January 19, 20.
Toss-Windward Islands. Match drawn.
MCC 124-5 (J.A.Jameson 39, G.Boycott 36 n.o.).
Windward Islands did not bat.

v West Indies Board of Control President's XI

4th Match
Played at Kensington Oval, Bridgetown, on January 23, 24, 25, 26.
Toss – MCC. Match drawn.

MCC

G. Boycott not out	261		
D. L. Amiss c Fredericks b Roberts	109		
J. A. Jameson lbw b Roberts	0	c and b Barrett	87
*M. H. Denness b Padmore	41		
K. W. R. Fletcher c Fredericks b Padmore	70		
†A. P. E. Knott	–	st Murray b Barrett	21
A. W. Greig	–	c Murray b Barrett	0
C. M. Old	–	c Foster b Barrett	19
P. I. Pocock	–	c and b Padmore	0
G. G. Arnold	–	not out	2
R. G. D. Willis	–		
Extras (b5, lb 2, nb 23)	30	(nb 2)	2
(4 wkts dec.)	511	(5 wkts dec.)	131

Fall: 252, 252, 343, 511

109, 109, 110, 121, 131

Bowling: Armstrong 26–2–106–0, Roberts 27–7–59–2, Holding 7–2–14–0, Padmore 51.3–9–149–2, Barrett 35–14–85–0, Foster 18–0–41–0, Fredericks 1–0–5–0, Greenidge 6–2–22–0

Second Innings: Armstrong 1–0–15–0, Roberts 7–1–32–0, Foster 7–3–15–0, Padmore 10–1–37–1, Fredericks 4–0–17–0, Barrett 6–3–13–4

President's XI

R. C. Fredericks c Greig b Arnold	0	c Amiss b Willis	8
C. G. Greenidge c Greig b Willis	37	c Jameson b Willis	28
L. Baichan b Arnold	49	not out	139
*M. L. C. Foster c Knott b Old	7	c Willis b Pocock	7
H. S. Chang b Willis	4	c Amiss b Pocock	64
†D. A. Murray c Jameson b Willis	8	b Willis	28
A. G. Barrett c Knott b Arnold	37	c Willis b Old	0
M. A. Holding c Old b Arnold	5	b Willis	1
A. Padmore c Amiss b Pocock	0	b Old	7
G. D. Armstrong lbw b Arnold	0	c Fletcher b Old	12
A. M. E. Roberts not out	0	not out	48
Extras (b 8, lb 1, nb 8)	17	(lb 8, nb 18)	26
	164	(9 wkts)	368

Fall: 1, 55, 63, 71, 85, 141, 155, 164, 164

10, 60, 171, 248, 250, 251, 252, 265, 284

Bowling: Willis 15–6–35–3, Arnold 12–5–44–5, Old 15–4–47–1, Pocock 6.1–0–21–1.

Second Innings: Willis 21–3–91–4. Arnold 18–4–73–0, Pocock 37–10–56–2, Old 23–8–56–3, Greig 15–3–53–0, Fletcher 4–1–13–0

Umpires: S. E. Parris and C. A. Vyfhuis

v Trinidad

5th Match
Played at Queen's Park Oval, Port of Spain, on January 28, 29, 30, 31. Toss — MCC. Match drawn.

MCC

G. Boycott b Julien	9	c Gabriel b Imtiaz Ali	4
D. L. Amiss c Durity b Imtiaz Ali	34	c Faria b Imtiaz Ali	8
J. A. Jameson c Gomes b Bartholemew	6	c Gabriel b Jumadeen	
F. C. Hayes b Imtiaz Ali	47	c Gabriel b Jumadeen	8
*M. H. Denness c Faria b Jumadeen	30	not out	2
K. W. R. Fletcher c Jumadeen b Bartholemew	18	lbw b Jumadeen	1
A. W. Greig lbw b Imtiaz Ali	70	not out	10
†A. P. E. Knott lbw b Julien	0	b Bartholemew	1
J. Birkenshaw not out	53		
D. L. Underwood lbw b Jumadeen	11		
M. Hendrick b Jumadeen	0		
Extras (b 4, lb 6, nb 5)	15	(b 5, lb 4, nb 3)	1
	293	(6 wkts)	**38**

Fall: 26, 35, 67, 121, 133, 182, 183, 246, 293   129, 136, 144, 178, 214, 303

Bowling: Bartholemew 22−4−57−2, Julien 18−3−49−2, Nanan 22−5−59−0, Imtiaz Ali 28−7−68−3, Jumadeen 23.5−7−45−3

Second Innings: Julien 11−2−27−0, Bartholemew 18−4−50−1, Jumadeen 50−14−81−3, Imtiaz Ali 25−4−98−2, Nanan 34−7−90−0, Faria 2−0−5−0, Gomes 4−0−21−0, Gabriel 1−0−3−0

Trinidad

R. A. Faria c Knott b Greig	63		
R. S. Gabriel c Knott b Greig	2		
O. M. Durity c Knott b Hendrick	8	Bowling:	Hendrick 21−5−62−3
S. A. Gomes b Greig	0		Greig 24−4−84−3
*†D. L. Murray c Hayes b Hendrick	148		Birkenshaw 39.2−10−82−3
B. D. Julien c Hayes b Birkenshaw	6		
C. Murray c Underwood b Birkenshaw	1		Underwood 34−14−48−1
P. C. S. Bartholemew c Knott b Hendrick	15		
R. Nanan lbw b Underwood	21		Fletcher 7−2−17−0
Imtiaz Ali not out	22		
R. R. Jumadeen b Birkenshaw	7		
Extras (b 2, lb 2, w 1, nb 14)	19		
	312		

Fall: 13, 37, 38, 148, 155, 164, 198, 236, 299

Umpires: R. Gosein and H. B. D. Jordan

160

West Indies (First Test)

6th Match
Played at Queen's Park Oval, Port of Spain, on February 2, 3, 5, 6, 7.
Toss — West Indies. West Indies won by 7 wickets.

England

G. Boycott c Julien b Boyce	6	c Fredericks b Gibbs	93
D. L. Amiss c Murray b Sobers	6	lbw b Sobers	174
*M. H. Denness b Julien	9	run out	44
F. C. Hayes c Fredericks b Sobers	12	b Sobers	8
K. W. R. Fletcher b Julien	4	c Rowe b Sobers	0
A. W. Greig c Murray b Boyce	37	b Gibbs	20
†A. P. E. Knott b Boyce	7	c Rowe b Gibbs	21
C. M. Old c Fredericks b Inshan Ali	11	c and b Gibbs	3
P.I. Pocock b Boyce	2	c Fredericks b Gibbs	0
D. L. Underwood not out	10	c Kanhai b Gibbs	9
R. G. D. Willis b Gibbs	6	not out	0
Extras (b 1, lb 8, nb 12)	21	(b 5, lb 5, nb 10)	20
	131		392

Fall: 6, 22, 23, 30, 71, 90, 100, 108, 116   209, 328, 338, 338, 349, 366,
378, 378, 391

Bowling: Boyce 19−4−42−4, Julien 12−5−14−2, Sobers 14−3−37−2,
Gibbs 3−1−5−1, Inshan Ali 7−5−12−1

Second Innings: Boyce 10−1−36−0, Julien 15−2−48−0, Sobers 34−15−54−3,
Gibbs 57.2−15−108−6, Inshan Ali 37−5−99−0, Fredericks 10−2−24−0,
Lloyd 3−1−3−0.

West Indies

R. C. Fredericks c Knott b Old	5	not out	65
L. G. Rowe c Knott b Willis	13	c Hayes b Pocock	5
A. I. Kallicharran c Underwood b Pocock	158	c Greig b Underwood	21
C. H. Lloyd c Denness b Old	18	c Hayes b Underwood	0
*R. B. Kanhai b Pocock	8	not out	39
G. St. A. Sobers c Denness b Underwood	23		
†D. L. Murray c Fletcher b Pocock	19		
B. D. Julien not out	86		
K. D. Boyce c Boycott b Pocock	26		
Inshan Ali c Knott b Pocock	9		
L. R. Gibbs b Old	2		
Extras (b 3, lb 6, nb 16)	25	(lb 1, nb 1)	2
	392	(3 wkts)	132

Fall: 14, 27, 63, 106, 147, 196, 296, 324, 373   15, 77, 77

Bowling: Willis 19−5−52−1, Old 20.4−2−89−3, Greig 17−3−60−0, Pocock
43−12−110−5, Underwood 23−8−56−1

Second Innings: Willis 4−1−6−0, Old 3−0−18−0, Pocock 16−6−49−1, Underwood
12−2−48−2, Greig 2−1−4−0, Fletcher 0.5−0−5−0

Batting times: England 1st innings: 227 min. 2nd innings: 502 min.
        West Indies 1st innings: 478 min. 2nd innings: 138 min.

Umpires: R. Gosein and D. Sang Hue.

v Jamaica

7th Match

Played at Sabina Park, Kingston, on February 9, 10, 12, 13. Toss — MCC.
Match drawn.

MCC

G. Boycott retired hurt	83	
J. A. Jameson c Lewis b Dowe	8	
*M. H. Denness c Headley b Rattigan	50	Bowling: Dowe 25.3–5–86–4
F. C. Hayes hit wkt b Dowe	30	Lawson 25–5–66–0
K. W. R. Fletcher c Foster b Dowe	107	Foster 19–10–20–0
A. W. Greig c Barrett b Gordon	20	Rattigan 32–5–75–1
A. P. E. Knott c Lewis b Gordon	5	Gordon 32–11–64–2
†R. W. Taylor st Lewis b Barrett	65	Barrett 35–8–81–2
G. G. Arnold b Barrett	0	
P. I. Pocock b Dowe	20	
M. Hendrick not out	4	
Extras (b 1, lb 1, nb 8)	10	
	402	

Fall: 10, 120, 184, 221, 229, 341, 341, 385, 402

Jamaica

L. G. Rowe lbw b Greig	41	b Jameson	118
S. Morgan c Jameson b Pocock	32	c Greig b Pocock	16
H. S. Chang c Boycott b Arnold	19	c Hayes b Boycott	22
*M. L. C. Foster b Pocock	1	lbw b Jameson	10
H. Gordon c Taylor b Greig	33		
†D. M. Lewis c Jameson b Pocock	23	not out	24
A. G. Barrett run out	0	not out	3
C. Lawson b Greig	4		
E. Rattigan b Hendrick	0		
U. G. Dowe not out	9		
R. G. A. Headley absent injured	–		
Extras (b 4, lb 1, nb 11)	16	(b 4, lb 1, nb 6)	11
	178	**(4 wkts)**	**204**

Fall: 69, 94, 96, 111, 151, 151, 155, 156, 178   43, 115, 137, 198

Bowling: Arnold 10–1–43–1, Hendrick 12–3–32–1, Pocock 24.2–5–45–3,
Greig 18–3–42–3

Second Innings: Arnold 13–4–38–0, Hendrick 9–2–28–0, Pocock 23–3–69–1,
Greig 3–0–8–0, Jameson 19–7–25–2, Boycott 8–1–25–1.

Umpires: K. Peart and D. Sang Hue.

The fourth Test at Georgetown. *Above* Jack Birkenshaw bowls Kallicharran for six. *Below* The author at work! The view from the commentary box at the Bourda Oval before rain washed out play.

Left Dennis Amiss, England's batsman of the series, plays an old-fashioned square-cut off the front foot during the final Test. Rohan Kanhai keeps wicket in the absence of the injured Murray; later he caught Amiss off Sobers.

Above A superhuman Tony Greig leaps across the wicket to catch Clive Lloyd off his own inspired bowling during the West Indian collapse on the last morning.

The crucial wicket on the pulsating final afternoon of the series.
Gary Sobers, in perhaps his last innings for the West Indies, is
bowled by Underwood—only the second time that this bowler
had ever taken the great man's wicket (the first occasion being
in the first Test).

v West Indies (Second Test)

8th Match
Played at Sabina Park, Kingston, on February 16, 17, 19, 20, 21.
Toss — England. Match drawn.

England

G. Boycott c Kanhai b Sobers	68	c Murray b Boyce	5
D. L. Amiss c Kanhai b Barrett	27	not out	262
J. A. Jameson st Murray b Gibbs	23	c Rowe b Barrett	38
F. C. Hayes c Boyce b Sobers	10	run out	0
*M. H. Denness c Fredericks b Boyce	67	c Rowe b Barrett	28
A. W. Greig c Fredericks b Barrett	45	b Gibbs	14
†A. P. E. Knott c Murray b Barrett	39	run out	6
C. M. Old c Murray b Julien	2	b Barrett	19
D. L. Underwood c Fredericks b Sobers	24	c Murray b Sobers	12
P. I. Pocock c Gibbs b Julien	23	c sub (Holder) b Boyce	4
R. G. D. Willis not out	6	not out	3
Extras (lb 7, nb 12)	19	(b 10, lb 11, w 1, nb 19)	41
	353	**(9 wkts)**	**432**

Fall: 68, 104, 133, 134, 224, 278, 286, 322, 333

32, 102, 107, 176, 217, 258, 271, 343, 392

Bowling: Boyce 19−2−52−1, Julien 18−3−40−2, Sobers 33−11−65−3,
Barrett 39−16−86−3, Gibbs 40−16−78−1, Fredericks 4−0−11−0, Lloyd 4−2−2−0

Second Innings: Julien 13−3−36−0, Boyce 21−4−70−2, Gibbs 44−15−82−1,
Barrett 54−24−87−3, Sobers 34−13−73−1, Fredericks 6−1−17−0, Lloyd 3−1−5−0,
Kanhai 3−1−8−0, Rowe 2−1−1−0, Kallicharran 3−0−12−0

West Indies

R. C. Fredericks b Old	94
L. G. Rowe lbw b Willis	120
A. I. Kallicharran c Denness b Old	93
C. H. Lloyd b Jameson	49
*R. B. Kanhai c Willis b Greig	39
G. St. A. Sobers c Willis b Greig	57
B. D. Julien c Denness b Greig	66
K. D. Boyce c Greig b Willis	8
†D. L. Murray not out	6
A. G. Barrett lbw b Willis	0
L. R. Gibbs not out	6
Extras (b 16, lb 18, nb 11)	45
(9 wkts dec.)	**583**

Bowling: Willis 24−5−97−3
Old 23−6−72−2
Pocock 57−14−152−0
Underwood 36−12−98−0
Greig 49−14−102−3
Jameson 7−2−17−1

Fall: 206, 226, 338, 401, 439, 551, 563, 567, 574

Batting times:
England 1st innings: 491 min.
2nd innings: 570 min.
West Indies 1st innings: 692 min.

Umpires: D. Sang Hue and H. B. D. Jordan

163

v Leeward Islands

9th Match
Played at Recreation Ground, St John's, Antigua, on February 23, 24, 2⁵
Toss — Leewards. Match drawn.

MCC

J. A. Jameson c and b Gore	28	lbw b Willett	
D. L. Amiss b Roberts	16	b V. Richards	
A. P. E Knott c M. Richards b Roberts	21	run out	
F. C. Hayes c Eddy b Corriette	40	not out	
K. W. R. Fletcher b Roberts	0	not out	
*A. W. Greig st Hector b Willett	45		
†R. W. Taylor lbw b Corriette	1	b Roberts	
J. Birkenshaw c Gore b Roberts	42		
G. G. Arnold c Sergeant b Willett	21		
M. Hendrick c Gore b Willett	16		
R. G. D. Willis not out	5		
Extras (b 12, nb 4)	16	(b 5)	
	251	(4 wkts dec.)1⁹	

Fall: 40, 46, 89, 89, 156, 157, 159, 214, 241   25, 34, 57, 82

Bowling: Roberts 24.3−4−75−4, Gore 12−2−39−1, Corriette 19−6−37−2,
Willett 30−7−55−3, V. A. Richards 9−2−15−0, Eddy 2−0−14−0

Second Innings: Roberts 19−2−65−1, Gore 3−0−5−0, Willett 21−8−33−1,
Corriette 17−7−37−0, V. A. Richards 7−1−25−1, Eddy 2−0−15−0,
M. Richards 1−0−5−0.

Leeward Islands

G. Yearwood run out	7	lbw b Birkenshaw	
V. Eddy c Greig b Arnold	45	b Hendrick	
J. C. Allen c and b Hendrick	0	c sub (Pocock) b Fletcher	
V. A. Richards c Hayes b Willis	42	not out	
L. C. Sergeant lbw b Willis	1		
M. Richards b Hendrick	30	b Hendrick	
A. Corriette lbw b Birkenshaw	32	c Taylor b Fletcher	
*†A. Hector c Jameson b Hendrick	17	not out	
E. T. Willett not out	0		
A. M. E. Roberts c Greig b Birkenshaw	2		
H. I. E. Gore b Hendrick	1		
Extras (b 4, lb 4, nb 9)	17	(b 4, lb 3, nb 9)	
	194	(5 wkts) 1	

Fall: 16, 81, 82, 121, 152, 153, 190, 190, 193   11, 108, 133, 145, 178

Bowling: Arnold 11−1−45−1, Willis 10−2−29−2, Hendrick 12.2−3−38−4,
Birkenshaw 10−1−39−2, Greig 8−1−26−0

Second Innings: Arnold 11−2−42−0, Hendrick 12−2−28−2, Birkenshaw 8−0−65
Greig 2−0−10−0, Fletcher 6−0−25−2, Jameson 2−0−7−0

Umpires: B. Roache and A. Syms

v Barbados

10th Match
Played at Kensington Oval, Bridgetown, on February 28, March 1, 2, 3.
Toss – Barbados. Barbados won by 10 wickets.

MCC

G. Boycott c Greenidge b Selman	2	c Greenidge b Selman	6
J. A. Jameson b Holford	91	hit wkt b Holder	9
*M. H. Denness c Lashley b Padmore	56	b Holder	5
F. C. Hayes c King b Holder	50	b Holder	10
K. W. R. Fletcher b Holford	2	lbw b Holder	23
†A. P. E. Knott c Greenidge b Padmore	10	lbw b Holder	39
C. M. Old b Padmore	0	c Padmore b King	53
G. G. Arnold c Holder b Armstrong	19	c Murray b Selman	25
D. L. Underwood c Padmore b Holder	12	c King b Selman	10
P. I. Pocock c Murray b Armstrong	4	b King	1
M. Hendrick not out	9	not out	0
Extras (b 3, nb 12)	15	(b 8, nb 10)	18
	270		**199**

Fall: 11, 146, 158, 163, 200, 200, 245, 245, 258

9, 25, 48, 84, 102, 107, 184, 198, 199

Bowling: Holder 19.2–5–45–2, Selman 4–0–21–1, Armstrong 14–1–46–2, King 6–0–29–0, Padmore 30–8–64–3, Holford 25–7–50–2

Second Innings: Holder 21–7–49–5, Selman 16–2–49–3, Armstrong 3–0–8–0, Holford 8–3–29–0, Padmore 4–0–38–0, King 2.2–0–8–2

Barbados

C. G. Greenidge c Knott b Pocock	36	not out	5
P. D. Lashley c Old b Hendrick	5	not out	6
N. E. Clarke c Jameson b Arnold	159		
C. L. King c Knott b Jameson	60		
†D. A. Murray c Knott b Underwood	57		
W. E. Ashby lbw b Underwood	61		
*D. A. J. Holford not out	52		
V. A. Holder c Hayes b Pocock	4		
C. A. Selman c Knott b Pocock	14		
A. Padmore not out	1		
G. D. Armstrong	–		
Extras (lb 3, nb 10)	13		0
(8 wkts dec.)	**462**	(no wkt)	**11**

Fall: 27, 80, 223, 292, 374, 419, 430, 447

Bowling: Arnold 24–7–95–1, Old 10–1–43–0, Hendrick 28–5–95–1, Pocock 36–11–103–3, Underwood 27–5–80–2, Jameson 7–1–25–1, Boycott 1–0–8–0

Second Innings: Hendrick 1–0–7–0, Hayes 0.2–0–4–0

Umpires: H. B. D. Jordan and S. E. Parris

v West Indies (Third Test)

11th Match
Played at Kensington Oval, Bridgetown, March 6, 7, 9, 10, 11. Toss —
West Indies. Match drawn.

England

*M. H. Denness c Murray b Sobers	... 24	lbw b Holder . . . . (
D. L. Amiss b Julien	12	c Julien b Roberts 4
J. A. Jameson c Fredericks b Julien	... 3	lbw b Roberts 9
G. Boycott c Murray b Julien	10	c Kanhai b Sobers 13
K. W. R. Fletcher c Murray b Julien	... 37	not out 129
A. W. Greig c Sobers b Julien	148	c Roberts b Gibbs 25
†A. P. E. Knott b Gibbs	87	lbw b Lloyd 67
C. M. Old c Murray b Roberts	1	b Lloyd . . . .
G. G. Arnold b Holder	12	not out 2
P. I. Pocock c Lloyd b Gibbs	18	
R. G. D. Willis not out	10	
Extras (lb 5 nb 28)	33	(b 7, lb 5, nb 16) 28
	395	(7 wkts) **27**

Fall: 28, 34, 53, 68, 130, 293, 306, 344, 371   4, 8, 29, 40, 106, 248, 248

Bowling: Holder 27−6−68−1, Roberts 33−8−75−1, Julien 26−9−57−5, Sobers 18−4−57−1, Gibbs 33.4−10−91−2, Lloyd 4−2−9−0, Fredericks 3−0−5−0

Second Innings: Holder 15−6−37−1, Roberts 17−4−49−2, Gibbs 28.3−15−40−1, Julien 11−4−21−0, Sobers 35−21−55−1, Lloyd 12−4−13−2, Fredericks 6−2−24− Rowe 1−0−5−0, Kallicharran 1−0−5−0

West Indies

R. C. Fredericks b Greig	32	
L. G. Rowe c Arnold b Greig	302	
A. I. Kallicharran b Greig	119	Bowling: Arnold 26−5−91−1
C. H. Lloyd c Fletcher b Greig	8	Willis 26−4−100−1
V. A. Holder c and b Greig	8	Greig 46−2−164−6
*R. B. Kanhai b Arnold	18	Old 28−4−102−0
G. St. A. Sobers c Greig b Willis	0	Pocock 28−4−93−0
†D. L. Murray not out	53	Batting times:
B. D. Julien c Willis b Greig	1	England 1st innings: 567 min.
A. M. E. Roberts not out	9	2nd innings: 405 min
L. R. Gibbs	−	West Indies 1st innings: 676 m
Extras (b 3, lb 8, nb 35)	46	
	(8 wkts dec.) **596**	

Fall: 126, 375, 390, 420, 465, 466, 551, 556

Umpires: D. Sang Hue and S. E. Parris.

v Guyana

12th Match
Played at Bourda Oval, Georgetown, on March 14, 15, 16, 17. Toss – Guyana. Match drawn.

Guyana

L. Baichan c Willis b Birkenshaw	71	c and b Willis	1
Romain Etwaroo c and b Underwood	25	c Taylor b Arnold	14
S. F. A. F. Bacchus b Hendrick	14	c Hendrick b Birkenshaw	24
R. C. Fredericks c Fletcher b Birkenshaw	112	not out	105
A. I. Kallicharran b Arnold	23	st Taylor b Birkenshaw	0
*C. H. Lloyd c Taylor b Birkenshaw	65	c Hayes b Underwood	24
†L. E. Skinner not out	27	c Taylor b Underwood	8
R. C. Collymore c Fletcher b Birkenshaw	0	run out	0
A. Persaud c Underwood b Birkenshaw	7	run out	6
P. D. Blair b Underwood	10	c Arnold b Fletcher	6
K. O. Cameron c Willis b Birkenshaw	6	not out	0
Extras (lb 6, nb 27)	33	(b 6, nb 8)	14
	393	(9 wkts dec.)	**202**

Fall: 81, 126, 127, 171, 341, 347, 347, 360, 382

1, 38, 40, 40, 81, 115, 123, 150, 200

Bowling: Arnold 21–3–72–1, Willis 18–1–90–0, Underwood 34–9–67–2, Hendrick 13–1–30–1, Birkenshaw 35.3–5–101–6

Second Innings: Arnold 5–2–11–1, Willis 3–0–26–1, Birkenshaw 33–10–84–2, Underwood 31–15–64–2, Fletcher 3–1–3–1

MCC

G. Boycott retired ill	133		
D. L. Amiss c Skinner b Fredericks	108	b Collymore	60
*M. H. Denness c Baichan b Persaud	7	not out	63
F. C. Hayes lbw b Blair	30	not out	8
K. W. R. Fletcher not out	26		
J. Birkenshaw not out	17		
Extras (b1, lb 1, w 1, nb 2)	5	(lb 7, nb 1)	8
(3 wkts dec.)	**326**	(1 wkt)	**139**

Did not bat: † R. W. Taylor, G. G. Arnold, D. L. Underwood, M. Hendrick, R. G. D. Willis.

Fall: 191, 208, 258

111

Bowling: Blair 18–2–79–1, Cameron 20–3–51–0, Collymore 36–8–89–0, Persaud 34–12–72–1, Fredericks 9–2–27–1, Lloyd 2–0–3–0

Second Innings: Blair 14–2–45–0, Cameron 6–0–24–0, Collymore 13–2–39–1, Persaud 6–1–23–0

Umpires: C. P. Kippins and C. A. Vyfhuis

v Guyana 2nd XI (not first-class)

13th Match
Played at Rose Hall Oval, Canje, Berbice, on March 19, 20. Toss —
Guyana 2nd XI. MCC won by 5 wickets.

Guyana 2nd XI 218—4 in 50 overs (L. Baichan 96, R. Gomes 61 n.o.,
L. Munilall 32) and 229—6d (R. R. Ramnarace 52, F. Hartman 52
n.o., L. Munilall 36, S. F. A. F. Bacchus 30).
MCC 211—4d in 44 overs (A. W. Greig 116, A. P. E. Knott 43,
S. Matthews 3—34) and 238—5 (J. A. Jameson 104, F. C. Hayes 62).
in 135 minutes.

v West Indies (Fourth Test)

14th Match
Played at Bourda Oval, Georgetown, on March 22, 23, 24, 26, 27.
Toss — England. Match drawn.

England

G. Boycott b Julien	15	
D. L. Amiss c Murray b Boyce	118	
*M. H. Denness b Barrett	42	Bowling: Boyce 27.4—6—70—3
K. W. R. Fletcher c Murray b Julien	41	Julien 36—10—96—2
A. W. Greig b Boyce	121	Lloyd 19—5—27—0
F. C. Hayes c and b Gibbs	6	Foster 16—5—32—0
†A. P. E. Knott c Julien b Gibbs	61	Gibbs 37—5—102—2
J. Birkenshaw c Murray b Fredericks	0	Barrett 31—6—87—1
C. M. Old c Kanhai b Boyce	14	Fredericks 5—2—12—1
G. G. Arnold run out	1	
D. L. Underwood not out	7	
Extras (b 1, lb 13, nb 8)	22	
	448	

Fall: 41, 128, 228, 244, 257, 376, 377, 410,
428

West Indies

R. C. Fredericks c and b Greig	98	
L. G. Rowe b Greig	28	Bowling: Arnold 10—5—17—0
A. I. Kallicharran b Birkenshaw	6	Old 13—3—32—0
*R. B. Kanhai b Underwood	44	Underwood 17.5—4—
C. H. Lloyd not out	7	36—1
Extras (b 6, lb 4, nb 5)	15	Greig 24—8—57—2
		Birkenshaw 22—7—41—
(4 wkts)	198	

Batting times:
England 628 min.
West Indies 336 min.

Fall: 73, 90, 179, 198

Did not bat: M. L. C. Foster, †D. L. Murray, B. D. Julien, K. D. Boyce, A. G. Barrett,
L. R. Gibbs

Umpires: D. Sang Hue and C. A. Vyfhuis

168

v West Indies (Fifth Test)

15th Match
Played at Queen's Park Oval, Port of Spain, on March 30, 31, April 2, 3, 4, 5. Toss — England. England won by 26 runs.

England

G. Boycott c Murray b Julien	99	b Gibbs	112
D. L. Amiss c Kanhai b Sobers	44	b Lloyd	16
*M. H. Denness c Fredericks b Inshan Ali	13	run out	4
K. W. R. Fletcher c Kanhai b Gibbs	6	b Julien	45
A. W. Greig lbw b Gibbs	19	c Fredericks b Julien	1
F. C. Hayes c Rowe b Inshan Ali	24	lbw b Julien	0
†A. P. E. Knott not out	33	lbw b Sobers	44
J. Birkenshaw c Lloyd b Julien	8	c Gibbs b Inshan Ali	7
G. G. Arnold run out	6	b Sobers	13
P. I. Pocock c Lloyd b Inshan Ali	0	c Kallicharran b Boyce	5
D. L. Underwood b Gibbs	4	not out	1
Extras (b 2, lb 3, nb 6)	11	(lb 4, nb 11)	15
	267		**263**

Fall: 83, 114, 133, 165, 204, 212, 244, 257, 260

39, 44, 145, 169, 174, 176, 213, 226, 258

Bowling: Boyce 10−3−14−0, Julien 21−8−35−2, Sobers 31−16−44−1, Inshan Ali 35−12−86−3, Gibbs 34.3−10−70−3, Lloyd 4−2−7−0

Second Innings: Sobers 24.2−9−36−2, Julien 22−7−31−3, Gibbs 50−15−85−1, Inshan Ali 34−12−51−1, Lloyd 7−4−5−1, Boyce 12−3−40−1

West Indies

R. C. Fredericks c Fletcher b Pocock	67	run out	36
L. G. Rowe c Boycott b Greig	123	lbw b Birkenshaw	25
A. I. Kallicharran c and b Pocock	0	c Fletcher b Greig	0
C. H. Lloyd c Knott b Greig	52	c and b Greig	13
G. St. A. Sobers c Birkenshaw b Greig	0	b Underwood	20
*R. B. Kanhai c and b Greig	2	c Fletcher b Greig	7
†D. L. Murray c Pocock b Greig	2	c Fletcher b Greig	33
B. D. Julien c Birkenshaw b Greig	17	c Denness b Pocock	2
K. D. Boyce c Pocock b Greig	19	not out	34
Inshan Ali lbw b Greig	5	c Underwood b Greig	15
L. R. Gibbs not out	0	b Arnold	1
Extras (b 11, lb 4, nb 3)	18	(b 9, lb 2, nb 2)	13
	305		**199**

Fall: 110, 122, 224, 224, 226, 232, 270, 300, 300

63, 64, 65, 84, 85, 135, 138, 166, 197

Bowling: Arnold 8−0−27−0, Greig 36.1−10−86−8, Pocock 31−7−86−2, Underwood 34−12−57−0, Birkenshaw 8−1−31−0

Second Innings: Arnold 5.3−1−13−1, Greig 33−8−70−5, Pocock 25−7−60−1, Birkenshaw 10−1−24−1, Underwood 15−7−19−1

Umpires: D. Sang Hue and S. Ishmael

Batting times: England 1st innings: 473 min. West Indies 1st innings: 448 min.
2nd innings: 481 min. 2nd innings: 336 min.

v Bermuda (not first-class)

16th Match
Played at National Stadium, Hamilton on April 7, 8, 9. Toss – MCC.
MCC won by an innings and 11 runs.

Bermuda

G. Brown c Jameson b Arnold	7	c Amiss b Underwood	31
S. Raynor c Taylor b Willis	45	c Hayes b Underwood	19
D. Morris c Taylor b Arnold	6	c Taylor b Underwood	11
S. Furbert c Hayes b Underwood	0	b Underwood	5
N. Gibbons b Willis	2	c Willis b Pocock	14
L. Raynor c and b Birkenshaw	32	c Taylor b Pocock	6
†D. Wainwright c Hayes b Pocock	14	c Pocock b Underwood	43
*J. Bailey c Jameson b Pocock	0	not out	10
E. Raynor not out	53	b Underwood	13
Shariz Ali b Birkenshaw	6	b Arnold	5
R. Simons b Birkenshaw	4	lbw b Pocock	1
Extras (lb 8, nb 4)	12	(b3, lb 2, nb 1)	6
	181		**164**

MCC

G. Boycott b Shariz Ali	131
D. L. Amiss c Wainwright b E. Raynor	33
J. A. Jameson c Brown b Shariz Ali	126
F. C. Hayes not out	58
*M. H. Denness	
J. Birkenshaw	
†R. W. Taylor	
G. G. Arnold	did not bat
P. I. Pocock	
D. L. Underwood	
R. G. D. Willis	
Extras (b 4, lb 4)	8
(3 wkts dec.)	**356**

MCC										Wkt	Bda	MCC	Bda
Arnold	15	3	47	2	7	2	20	1			1st	1st	2nd
Willis	18	7	46	2	5	0	28	0		1st	33	59	6
Underwood	20	6	40	1	21	9	33	6		2nd	45	246	86
Pocock	5	0	18	2	17.1	8	26	3		3rd	54	356	86
Birkenshaw	6.2	2	18	3	12	1	51	0		4th	70		107
										5th	72		107
Bermuda										6th	99		12
Simons	23	0	97	0						7th	105		142
L. Raynor	8	1	43	0						8th	153		141
Shariz Ali	29	5	94	2						9th	169		163
Bailey	11	0	55	0						10th	181		164
E. Raynor	11	1	44	1									
Furbert	3	0	15	0									

Umpires: W. Davies and K. Parris

v Somerset Cricket Club (not first-class)

17th Match
Played at Somerset Cricket Club Ground, Bermuda, on April 10. Toss
– MCC. Match drawn.

MCC 201–7 (J. A. Jameson 53, K. W. R. Fletcher 51, A. W. Greig
37 n.o., D. Richardson 3–42).

Rain stopped play. Somerset did not bat.

4 A statistician's diary

Combined Islands — Castries, St Lucia
The tenth official MCC tour of the West Indies began with a defeat in the first-ever fixture between MCC and a Combined Leeward-Windward Islands team. This was also MCC's first defeat in any non-first-class match in the West Indies.

Windward Islands — Castries, St Lucia
The only previous instance of an MCC match being abandoned without a ball being bowled in the West Indies occurred in February 1948 when rain prevented any play in the second match against British Guiana at Georgetown.

West Indies Board of Control President's XI — Bridgetown, Barbados
G. Boycott's innings of 261 not out was the highest of his career (beating his 260 not out for Yorkshire against Essex at Colchester in 1970), and his partnership of 252 with D. L. Amiss (109) was the third-highest for MCC's (or England's) first wicket in the Caribbean; the two higher stands being:

322 G. Gunn and A. Sandham v Jamaica at Kingston in 1929-30

281 G. Pullar and M. C. Cowdrey v British Guiana at Georgetown in 1959-60

For the first time in the West Indies, MCC batsmen shared century opening partnerships in both innings:

First innings — 252 G. Boycott and D. L. Amiss

Second innings — 109 J. A. Jameson and A. P. E. Knott

First Test — Port of Spain, Trinidad
M. H. Denness became the first player born in Scotland to captain England in an official Test Match.

Greig's running-out of Kallicharran: it is quite without precedent for an appeal upheld in a Test Match to be withdrawn — and, in consequence, for an umpire to revoke his decision — *as a result of a lengthy off-the-field conference between captains, administrators and umpires.*

Instances of appeals being withdrawn and umpires revoking their original decisions have occurred in Test cricket:

1950–51   New Zealand v England at Christchurch – C. Washbrook was given out l.b.w. but W. A. Hadlee, New Zealand's captain, felt certain that the ball had hit bat before pad, consulted the umpire and recalled the batsman who resumed his innings.

1964–65   South Africa v England at Johannesburg – M. J. K. Smith went down the pitch 'gardening' after failing to play a ball which wicket-keeper J. H. B. Waite tossed to P. L. van der Merwe at leg-slip. That fielder threw down the wicket and umpire H. C. Kidson, after giving Smith out (run out), was prevailed upon by South Africa's captain, T. L. Goddard, to change his decision and recall the batsman.

Three other instances of unusual run-outs have occurred in Test Matches:

1882   England v Australia at The Oval – S. P. Jones, after responding to a call for a single and completing the run, indulged in some mid-pitch 'gardening' and was run out by W. G. Grace.

1947–48   Australia v India at Sydney – W. A. Brown, the non-striker, was run out by the bowler, V. Mankad, for backing up before the ball had been bowled.

1960   England v South Africa at Nottingham – D. J. McGlew, the non-striker, collided with the bowler, A. E. Moss, as the latter dashed across the wicket to field the ball. McGlew failed to reach his crease and was given out by umpire C. S. Elliott from square-leg. Although England's captain, M. C. Cowdrey, recalled McGlew, the umpire refused to change his decision.

P. I. Pocock (5 for 110) became the third England bowler to take five wickets in an innings of a Port of Spain Test; the others being:

W. Voce   7 for 70 in 1929-30

F. S. Trueman 5 for 35 in 1959-60

D. L. Underwood dismissed G. St. A. Sobers for the first time in any first-class match.

The partnership of 209 between G. Boycott (93) and D. L. Amiss (174) set a new record for England's first wicket in the West Indies, beating 177 by M. C. Cowdrey and G. Pullar at Kingston in 1959-60. It was just three runs short of England's record opening stand against West Indies: 212 by C. Washbrook and R. T. Simpson at Nottingham in 1950.

L. R. Gibbs became the first bowler to take 250 Test wickets for West Indies when he dismissed A. W. Greig in the second innings. His analysis of 6 for 108 was his 15th instance of five or more wickets in a Test innings and his seventh against England.

For the first time in 68 Test innings C. H. Lloyd was dismissed for nought.

R. B. Kanhai became the third West Indies captain to win a Test after winning the toss and inviting the opposition to bat; the others being:

F. M. M. Worrell v India at Bridgetown in 1961-62

G. St. A. Sobers v New Zealand at Auckland in 1968-69

Defeat by seven wickets ended England's unbeaten run of 13 Tests in the West Indies since L. Hutton's team lost the Second Test of 1953-54. It also ended a dismal run of 22 home Tests without victory for West Indies.

Second Test — Kingston, Jamaica
The partnership of 206 between R. C. Fredericks (94) and L. G. Rowe (120) set a new first-wicket record for West Indies against England, beating 173 by G. M. Carew and A. G. Ganteaume at Port of Spain in 1947-48. Fredericks scored his 2,000th run in Tests when he reached 44.

During his innings of 57, G. St. A. Sobers completed an unique double of 8,000 runs and 200 wickets in 91 Tests for West Indies.

West Indies innings of 583 for 9 dec. included three hundred-partnerships; their only previous similar instance against England was at Nottingham in 1966.

D. L. Amiss's innings of 262 not out was the highest of his career, the eighth-highest for England and the third-highest by an English batsman in the West Indies after:

325   A.Sandham v West Indies at Kingston in 1929-30

281 n.o. W. R. Hammond v Barbados at Bridgetown in 1934-35

Amiss batted 570 minutes, faced 563 balls and hit a six and 40 fours. He reached 50 in 93 minutes, 100 in 192 minutes, 150 in 334 minutes, 200 in 446 minutes and 250 in 549 minutes. It was his first double-century in first-class cricket and only an unbeaten innings lasting 53 minutes by England's last man, R. G. D. Willis, prevented his joining the select list of batsmen who have carried their bat through a completed Test innings.

Between 2nd March 1973 and 21st February 1974, Amiss scored 1,356 runs in Test Matches at an average of 79.76; a feat especially remarkable considering that his first ten England caps were spread over seven different series.

P.I. Pocock batted for 83 minutes in scoring four singles off 88 balls.

Third Test — Bridgetown, Barbados
A. M. E. Roberts became the first Antiguan to play in a Test Match. R. B. Kanhai became the first West Indies captain to twice invite the opposition to bat in the same series.

A. W. Greig (148) equalled his highest Test score and, with A. P. E. Knott (whose 87 was his highest score against West Indies), added 163 to set a new England sixth-wicket record against West

Indies, beating 161 by T. E. Bailey and T. G. Evans at Manchester in 1950.

L. G. Rowe's innings of 302 was the highest of his career, his eleventh first-class century but his first outside Sabina Park, the highest score for West Indies against England (beating 270 not out by G. A. Headley at Kingston in 1934-35), the eleventh triple-century in Test cricket and the second (after Sobers's 365 not out) by a West Indian. Rowe batted for 612 minutes, faced 430 balls and hit a six and 36 fours. He reached 50 in 88 minutes, 100 in 207 minutes, 150 in 300 minutes, 200 in 415 minutes, 250 in 512 minutes and 300 in 605 minutes.

Rowe's stand of 249 with A. I. Kallicharran (119) set a new West Indies record for the second wicket against England, beating 228 by R. K. Nunes and G. A. Headley at Kingston in 1929-30.

A. W. Greig (148 and 6 for 164) became the first England player to score a century and take five wickets in an innings of the same Test Match. There had been only four previous instances in Test cricket of a player scoring a century and taking **six** wickets:

J. H. Sinclair	106 & 6 for 26	S. Africa v England (Cape Town)	1898-99
J. M. Gregory	100 & 7 for 69	Australia v England (Melbourne)	1920-21
K. R. Miller	109 & 6 for 107	Australia v W. Indies (Kingston)	1954-55
G. St. A. Sobers	183 & 6 for 21	Rest of World v England (Lord's)	1970

K. W. R. Fletcher's 18th run was his 2,000th for England. Against Trinidad earlier on the tour he had reached 20,000 runs in first-class cricket.

The match produced 99 calls of 'no-ball' (runs being scored off 20 of them) — a record for any Test. England's bowlers were called 47 times in West Indies' only innings, 35 appearing as extras — both Test records.

Guyana — Georgetown

R. C. Fredericks (112 and 105 not out) became the second batsman to score two hundreds in a match against MCC/England in the West Indies. The first was G. A. Headley who scored 114 and 112 in the Third Test at Georgetown in 1929-30. This was the third time that Fredericks had achieved this feat for Guyana at the Bourda ground; he scored 127 and 115 against Barbados in 1966-67 and 158 and 118 against the Australians in 1972-73.

For the second time on the tour MCC batsmen shared century opening stands in both innings:

First innings — 191 G. Boycott and D. L. Amiss

Second innings — 111 M. H. Denness and D. L. Amiss

Fourth Test — Georgetown, Guyana

This was England's 500th Test Match, the first having begun on 15th March 1877 against Australia at Melbourne. To cheer the statisticians, M. H. Denness won the 250th toss for England. After rain and poor drainage had reduced the match by 13 hours and 26 minutes and made a draw inevitable, England's record read:

Opponents	Won	Lost	Drawn	Total
Australia	70	82	62	214
South Africa	46	18	38	102
West Indies	20	19	26	65
New Zealand	22	0	23	45
India	19	6	20	45
Pakistan	9	1	14	24
Rest of the World	1	4	0	5
Totals	187	130	183	500

D. L. Amiss (118) reached 1,000 runs in first-class matches on the tour when he had scored 58. He became the first England player to score three hundreds in a series against West Indies.

A. P. E. Knott (61) scored his third successive fifty of the series and shared in a century stand for England's sixth wicket for the third innings in succession.

Fifth Test — Port of Spain, Trinidad

England took first innings for the fifth time in the series. This was the sixth instance of one side taking first innings throughout a five-match rubber:

England v Australia	1905
West Indies v India	1948-49
England v West Indies	1959-60
England v South Africa	1960
West Indies v England	1966

G. St. A. Sobers became the first bowler to take 100 wickets for West Indies against another country when he dismissed D. L. Amiss in the first innings. L. R. Gibbs emulated this feat in the second innings when he took the wicket of G. Boycott.

C. H. Lloyd reached 1,000 runs for West Indies against England when he had scored 48.

A. W. Greig's first innings analysis of 8 for 86 set a new record for bowlers of either side in England—West Indies Tests, beating 8 for 104 by A. L. Valentine for West Indies at Manchester in 1950 (his Test debut) and 7 for 34 by T. E. Bailey at Kingston in 1953-54.

D. L. Amiss (663) returned the third-highest series aggregate for England against West Indies (E. H. Hendren 693 in 1929-30 and L. Hutton 677 in 1953-54). Only D. C. S. Compton (753 v South

Africa in 1947) and L. Hutton had scored more runs in a post-war series for England.

Amiss's tour aggregate of 1,120 in first-class matches was the fourth-highest for MCC after E. H. Hendren's 1,765 and A. Sandham's 1,281 in 1929-30, and G. Boycott's 1,154 in 1967-68.

G. Boycott (99 and 112) failed by one run to become the first England batsman to score a hundred in both innings against West Indies. In 1959-60 M. C. Cowdrey scored 114 and 97 at Kingston.

R. C. Fredericks equalled Sobers's West Indies record of 10 catches in a series against England, set in 1966, when he caught A. W. Greig in the second innings.

A. W. Greig's match analysis of 13 for 156 was the best of his first-class career and the best for England since 1956 when J. C. Laker took 19 for 90 against Australia at Manchester. It also set a new record in England–West Indies Tests, beating 12 for 119 by F. S. Trueman at Birmingham in 1963 and 11 for 147 by K. D. Boyce at The Oval in 1973.

This was only the seventh Test to be decided out of the last 27 played in the West Indies. Of those seven, six have been at Queen's Park Oval.

Man of the Series
A. W. GREIG, who failed by only one wicket to become the first England player to achieve the rare double of 250 runs and 25 wickets in a series; a feat which eluded many fine all-rounders including Sobers and Hammond:

	Runs	*Wkts*		
G. Giffen	475	34	Australia v England	1894–95
G. A. Faulkner	545	29	South Africa v England	1909–10
R. Benaud	329	30	Australia v South Africa	1957–58
T. L. Goddard	294	26	South Africa v Australia	1966–67

Nevertheless, Greig's performance in scoring 430 runs (av. 47.77) with two hundreds, taking 24 wickets (av. 22.62), and holding 7 catches undoubtedly represented the finest all-round achievement in any series played in the West Indies.